Praise for Alison Green and *Ask a Manager*

"*Ask a Manager* is the ultimate playbook for navigating the traditional workforce in a diplomatic but firm way. Alison Green covers just about every conceivable awkward moment you can (and will) experience as an employee, coworker, or boss and gives you a script for how to address and, more important, solve the problem."

—Erin Lowry, author of *Broke Millennial: Stop Scraping By and Get Your Financial Life Together*

"*Ask a Manager* is essential reading for anyone who has to navigate the weirdness of office culture, managers who are possibly unhinged, or the dreaded coworker who will *just not stop talking*. Alison Green is the workplace mentor you always wanted—wise, kind, and unflappable."

—Jolie Kerr, author of *My Boyfriend Barfed in My Handbag . . . And Other Things You Can't Ask Martha*

"This book should be required reading for anyone who manages or is managed—or often feels like the only one who has ever had a bad coworker or needed to give notice or asked for a raise. This book handles just about every work conundrum you've ever stayed up late at night worried about. I'd recommend reading it . . . and then conspicuously leaving it in your break room. Green is the work guru we've been reading for years: Of course her book is fantastic!"

—Alida Nugent, author of *Don't Worry, It Gets Worse* and *You Don't Have to Like Me*

"Clear and concise in its advice and expansive in its scope, *Ask a Manager* is the book I wish I'd had in my desk drawer when I was starting out (or even, let's be honest, fifteen years in). Alison Green's pragmatic approach to solving workplace dilemmas—from taking criticism to dishing it out—will not only make you a better, happier employee, it will help you tolerate less-than-perfect managers and put you well on your way to having their job someday . . . and doing it better."

—SARAH KNIGHT, *New York Times* bestselling author of *The Life-Changing Magic of Not Giving a F*ck, Get Your Sh*t Together,* and *You Do You*

"As someone who has lost (*happily devoted,* rather) countless hours of her life to committing the Ask a Manager archives to memory, I've been ready for this book for years, in some ways since birth. In some ways I have been genetically coded to have this book in my life since I was born. I don't know anything about having a job, and Alison Green knows so much; she always seems to have the perfect thing to say, the balance between tact and firmness. Every time I think, 'This is it, this is the Unsolvable Problem, there is nothing anyone could possibly say to address this broken situation,' Green will toss out four or five perfect short sentences, and I'll think, 'Oh, yeah, that'll do it.' This book does it."

—MALLORY ORTBERG, author of *Texts from Jane Eyre* and *The Merry Spinster*

"Alison Green is the resource I wish I'd had as a young worker bee. Her advice is sage, straightforward, and empathetic."

—ANDI ZEISLER, cofounder of Bitch Media

Ask a Manager

Ask a Manager

How to Navigate Clueless Colleagues, Lunch-Stealing Bosses, and the Rest of Your Life at Work

Alison Green

BALLANTINE BOOKS
NEW YORK

Published in the United States by Ballantine Books,
an imprint of Random House, a division of Penguin Random House LLC, New York.

BALLANTINE and the HOUSE colophon are registered trademarks
of Penguin Random House LLC.

Some letters and answers have previously appeared on the author's blog, askamanager.org.
In addition, the letter "My coworker wants us to call her boyfriend her 'master'"
and answer on page 142 was originally published in "Ask a Boss" at
New York magazine's The Cut.

ISBN 9780399181818
Ebook ISBN 9780399181825

Printed in the United States of America on acid-free paper

randomhousebooks.com

987654321

First Edition

Book design by Diane Hobbing

Interior illustrations by Kate Taylor

To M., who signed up for
a lifetime of weird conversations

Contents

Ask a Manager

Introduction

More than a decade ago, I started a workplace advice column, Ask a Manager. At the time, I was working as the chief of staff for a nonprofit lobbying organization, and I kept seeing people make choices at work that didn't produce the outcomes they wanted. It occurred to me that people could use a place where they could get a manager's perspective on their work problems, and thus Ask a Manager was born. I figured I'd mainly be answering questions about writing a résumé, asking for a raise, adjusting to a new boss, and other basic aspects of having a job.

Little did I know I'd end up spending most of my time fielding much more nuanced questions about how to talk to each other at work—from what to say to a coworker who won't stop texting you, to what to do when you're allergic to a colleague's perfume, to how to deal with a boss who steals your lunch (seriously).

It turns out that our workplaces are full of people who are frustrated, hurt, or fed up—but aren't speaking up about it because they can't figure out what to say or even how to start the conversation. And when people don't know exactly how to say something at work, they often end up saying nothing at all . . . causing their irritation to fester and grow and leaving the problem unresolved.

I know this because I now receive around sixty letters a day at Ask a Manager from people asking for help with workplace interactions ranging from the mundane to the truly bizarre.

And let's be clear: I'm not a perfect manager or colleague. I've made lots and lots of mistakes, and I definitely don't have all the answers. But in a decade of running Ask a Manager, I've had to think through a wide—and weird—range of interpersonal issues that arise at work and, in particular, what to say when you need to talk about them.

Surprisingly often, the answers to the questions that my letter writers ask come down to this: *Speak up*. That's often all that's needed—a conversation. But the reason people don't take that step is that they have no fricking clue what to say.

And that's understandable. Your job is your livelihood, so of course you're wary of injecting tension or weirdness into your encounters with colleagues. Your quality of life at work often depends on having a decent relationship with your coworkers and (especially) with your boss, who controls everything from what work assignments you get to whether you'll still have a job next week. So, yes, the stakes are high.

But the stakes are high if you *don't* speak up, too. When the issue is serious—for example, if you're not getting paid on time—not speaking up could mean not being able to pay your bills. But even when the issue isn't so crucial—even when it's, say, asking your coworker to turn his music down or to stop calling you "m'lady"—not speaking up means not having perfectly reasonable conversations, in the name of avoiding minor awkwardness. If you speak up—not adversarially, not aggressively, just calmly and matter-of-factly—you'll build a reputation as someone who's able to navigate tough situations with relative grace. You'll also significantly improve your quality of life at work, because when you speak up appropriately, you improve your working conditions and relationships. (You also might find that those skills are transferable to life outside of work, which is an added bonus.)

By the way, the "not adversarially" part is pretty crucial. While loads of people choose not to speak up at all and suffer in silence, I've also watched too many people speak up badly. They're too aggressive and they come in too hot, and as a result their perfectly legitimate concerns are lost in the messaging.

So in this book, I'm going to give you suggested language to help you navigate all sorts of situations at work, and tell you exactly how to say the thing you'd like to say.

As you read, keep in mind these three principles:

1. **There is no magic wand.** I hear from a lot of people whose questions boil down to, "My coworker is doing Annoying Thing X" (e.g., taking all her calls on speakerphone, dumping last-minute work on me as I'm walking out the door at night, spitting on me while she talks, etc.). "How can I get her to stop without actually saying anything to her about it?" And, sure, of course we want people to stop annoying us without needing to have an awkward conversation. I want that too! But in the vast majority of cases, that's not really an option.

It's true that in *some* cases, the annoying behavior is egregious enough that you can skip talking to the person directly and go straight to their manager or HR. But those cases are the exception, not the rule. You definitely don't want to go to

HR about your coworker who spits when he talks. You'll look like you can't manage your own work relationships, and they're likely to tell you to go back and talk to your coworker directly anyway.

In most cases, if someone is doing something that upsets or annoys you, and you want her to stop, the only way to make that happen is to speak up and tell her so. So you have to decide: Are you willing to speak up and have the conversation? Or do you want to avoid that conversation so much that you're willing to continue putting up with the behavior that's bugging you? Those are usually your only two choices.

2. **Most people are reasonable.** Most people want to know if they're doing something that's annoying the crap out of you. Most managers want to know if someone on their staff is deeply unhappy about something. Most people won't be upset that you initiated the conversation, and you aren't going to come across as a jerk to reasonable people.

Because of that, speaking up will usually go better than you think it will. But we should be realistic. In some cases, the conversation might cause tension or awkwardness or make someone angry with you. These things happen! They happen less often than people fear, but they're certainly possible outcomes. In this book, I'm going to give you language that will make a bad outcome much less likely. Of course, you can't control everything, and some people are unreasonable loons, but most of the time the worst thing that will happen is some fleeting awkwardness, followed by a return to normalcy.

3. *How* **you speak up is key.** Your tone and the way you frame the conversation will play a huge part in determining the outcome.

In these conversations, you should sound calm, matter-of-fact, and collaborative. Think of the tone that you'd use if you were trying to solve a work-related problem with a colleague and you *hadn't* spent the last two nights lying awake, mustering the nerve to initiate the conversation. That's the tone you're aiming for.

SO LET'S DIVE in and start navigating the awkward, the tricky, and the just plain weird issues that you might run into at work.

Are there times when you shouldn't speak up at all?

While I passionately want people to get more comfortable speaking up at work, there are plenty of times when speaking up wouldn't be the right call, such as:

- **When you lack standing or capital.** Everyone at work has a certain amount of social and professional capital to spend. How much you have is based on how long you've worked at your company, how senior your position is, how well you generally get along with people, how much your work is valued, how much your boss likes you personally, and how accommodating you've been to others. If you're low on accumulated capital, you might not be well positioned to speak up about a difficult or sensitive issue. (There are exceptions to this rule when it comes to things that are very serious. For example, you should always speak up about sexual harassment or unsafe working conditions.)

- **When you have bigger battles to fight.** If you're asking for a raise and better project assignments, now probably isn't the time to also ask your boss to stop taking all her calls on speakerphone. Focus on what's most important to you, and don't overreach.

- **When you just want to say something because it would feel good but there's no benefit beyond that.** As a fan since birth of speaking up just on principle, I'm sympathetic to this one. It can feel really satisfying to voice something that's been bothering you, even if it's not going to achieve anything, even if it might actually make the situation worse. But at work, you have to weigh that satisfaction against the impact it's likely to have on your relationships in the office, and possibly on your professional reputation, too.

  Of course, you may weigh those factors and still decide you want to say something. If so, that's your call! Just make sure that you do the calculation first.

- **When the timing is bad.** If the person you want to talk to is on a tight deadline, dealing with a family crisis, or just spoke to you about serious problems with your work, it's probably not the right time to raise something difficult or sticky if it could otherwise wait.

CHAPTER 1

Conversations with Your Boss

Conversations with your boss can be stressful even when they're relatively routine. The uneven power dynamic can mess with your head and make you approach conversations far more delicately than you need to, or even convince you not to have the conversation at all.

But for the most part, you'll get the best results if you approach your boss as if she's a normal human, not royalty or a terrible ogre. That's sometimes easier said than done, though, so here are some general operating instructions to follow:

- **Don't overthink it.** Overthinking will cause you a lot more stress and anxiety than is probably warranted and it's likely to make you less effective, too. You'll wind up dancing around the issue, or using formal wording that sounds odd and unclear. Just be direct and straightforward.

- **Keep your ego at bay.** The more you can approach the conversation from an emotionally detached place, the more effective you're likely to be. This doesn't mean that you can't have emotions; it just means that you can't let them drive the conversation. For example, if your boss gives you some critical feedback and you get defensive or upset, you're less likely to truly process the guidance she's giving you. Instead, calmly ask for more information and talk through your options. That should lead you away from defensive responses like "No one told me not to do it that way!" and toward more constructive responses like "Would it be better to do X?" or "I think X is happening because of Y. Let me try Z and see if that solves it."

- **Think like a consultant.** Employees' relationships with their managers sometimes resemble a parent/child dynamic more than a peer-to-peer relationship—and that's not a good thing. To avoid that, try thinking of yourself as a consultant and your boss as your client. Consultants are able to sidestep that parent-child dynamic because they're independently offering their services, and while they want to make their clients happy, if they ultimately can't see eye to eye on something important, they can part ways without a ton of drama. And really, that's true for employees, too—employees just tend to lose sight of it.

- **When you bring concerns to your boss, frame them from the perspective of "What makes the most sense for the organization and why?" rather than "I want X."** The former is the perspective that your boss will need to take, so it's better for both of you if the conversation starts there. However . . .

- **If something really just comes down to "I want X," it's okay to be straightforward about that.** If you're in pretty good standing with your boss and you have some credibility built up (in part because you don't approach her with "I want X"-type requests on a daily basis), then sometimes it's okay to say, "I know that this doesn't sound like a big deal, but it's driving me crazy. Could we try doing X instead?" or "X is really important to me. Can we talk about whether there's any way to make that happen?" Good bosses want to make good employees happy, so knowing what would make you happier is actually great information for them to have.

- **Make it clear that you understand that your boss may have different information or a different perspective than you.** In many cases, your boss really *will* have more information than you do, and you should approach sensitive conversations with that in mind. For example, if you're concerned about why your boss moved a high-profile project from you to your co-worker, start by saying, "I realize that there might be reasons for this that I'm not privy to" as opposed to just launching into "I'm really upset about losing this project." You'll have more credibility, and you won't put your boss on the defensive.

- **In some cases you'll get better results by asking for a short-term experiment rather than a permanent change.** If your boss is resistant to what you're asking for, suggesting a short-term trial rather than a permanent change can be a good way to lower the stakes. For example, if you want to work from home on Thursdays and your boss isn't convinced it makes sense, she might agree more easily if you don't ask her to commit to it forever. Instead, say, "Could we try it for the next three Thursdays and see how it goes? If it causes problems, of course I wouldn't continue. But it could be a good way to test it out." This approach works for all kinds of requests, from asking for more autonomy in your work to suggesting a different format for staff meetings.

1. Your boss seems unhappy with your work

Sometimes it's clear that your boss is unhappy with your work: You're getting a lot of critical feedback and/or she tells you directly that she's concerned. Other times, you might be less certain. Maybe you have a vague sense that she's dissatisfied without having anything concrete to point to, or you might not know whether the amount of criticism you're getting is par for the course or something to worry about.

In all these cases, the worst thing you can do is silently worry. You might think that raising the issue will make it worse, but really, if your boss has concerns about your performance, it's much better to know and to try to address the situation. If you avoid the topic, you won't ever know what you could be doing better. And you might be denying yourself peace of mind, too, if in fact your boss isn't as worried as you think.

So, name what you're worried about and ask for more insight. Here are some ways you can say it:

- *"I'm getting the sense that you're concerned about how I'm handling X and Y. If so, I'd really like to talk it through with you and get your feedback."*

- *"I might be misreading, but you seemed disappointed with how project X went. Could we talk about how you think it went?"*

- *"Can I ask about some of the feedback you've given me lately? I wasn't sure if this is the amount and type of feed-*

back you'd normally expect to give the person in my role, or if I'm having a tougher time than you'd generally expect."

- *"Could we talk about how things are going overall? I'd really like to get your feedback on how I'm doing, in the big picture."*

2. The job isn't what you agreed to

If you find yourself in a new job that's significantly different from the one you signed up for, you should speak up. First, if you don't speak up, your boss may not even realize this is happening; he may be so busy with other things that he hasn't fully focused on what's going on with you. Second, you want to find out whether you're just pinch-hitting for someone else short-term (maybe until someone has time to train you on your primary responsibilities or until something else changes) or this is what the job will look like long-term. And third, you need to be clear that you're not okay with doing a different job than the one you signed up for. (Don't assume that this is obvious.)

Start by saying something like this:

- *"Since I started a month ago, I've been spending most of my time on database maintenance. Could we talk about the plan for getting the accounting work transferred over to me? I was happy to help out with the database because I know we were in a pinch with Niles being out, but I'd really like to focus on the accounting work I was hired for."*

If your manager says that there are no immediate plans to make that happen, you could say:

- *"Would you be open to talking about handling it differently? I hadn't expected the job to be centered on database work when I took it, and it's not something I'd normally seek to make part of my role."*

It's possible that this conversation will make your manager realize that he needs a different plan—in which case, great, problem solved. But it's also possible that you'll hear, "Yeah, I'm sorry it worked out this way, but this is what we need from the role now." If that's the case, you'll need to decide if you want the job under these new terms. That's definitely not fair—but if it's the reality of the situation, it's better to figure that out sooner rather than later so that you can decide how you want to proceed.

3. You have concerns about a colleague's work

Let's say you have a coworker who isn't very good at her job. Her work is full of mistakes, or she doesn't return calls from her clients so they end up contacting you for help instead, or she's frequently late in finishing up her piece of a joint project.

A lot of people will tell you that if the problems aren't impacting your ability to do your own job, you should stay out of it. And sometimes that's true—if the problems are minor. But if the problems are significant and you can see that they're affecting your team or your organization, a good manager will appreciate a discreet heads-up about what's going on.

Of course, "significant" is the key here. Your coworker coming in two minutes late every day probably doesn't meet that bar, but clients complaining that your coworker never responds to their calls probably does. The question to ask yourself is: How does this affect our work, and by how much? If it's more than mildly annoying and has a real impact on the work, a good boss will want to know about it.

And of course, if the problems are affecting *your* work, it's all the more imperative to say something.

When you do this, just be direct and stick to the facts. Explain what's going on, what the impact has been, and ideally what you're hoping your manager might do in response.

For example, when a coworker misses deadlines that affect you, here are a few ways to let your boss know:

- *"I wanted to mention to you that the last few times we've had proposal deadlines, I've had to work late to get everything done at the last minute because Oswald's portions keep coming to me late. I've asked him to get his work to me earlier, but that hasn't resolved it. Could you nudge him to hit our internal deadlines more reliably?"*

A slightly sneakier way of tipping off your manager about a problem with a coworker is to *ask for advice* about dealing with that problem. That way you're alerting her to what's happening without having to worry that you're coming across as a complainer. For example:

- *"Can I ask for your advice about how to handle something? I'm getting a lot of calls from Oswald's clients after they've left messages for him and not heard anything back. When they don't get a response for a few days, they'll sometimes call me to try to get help, but I don't have all the info on their accounts. I've let Oswald know this is happening, but it hasn't resolved it. Can you give me some advice on the best way to handle this?"*

And if the problems don't directly affect your work but still feel important enough to raise, try saying something like this:

• *"I wanted to mention that I've overheard Oswald giving callers some incorrect info about our work. For example, he gave one person the wrong website address and told someone else that we don't accept credit card payments over the phone even though we do. I gave him the right information both times I overheard, but I think he might need more training on answering common questions from callers."* (Note that the framing here isn't "Let's get Oswald in trouble!" but rather "Here's a work problem that might need some attention.")

By the way, in many cases, you should first try to resolve the problem with your coworker directly. Most people appreciate the chance to fix something themselves before their boss is involved. But if you've tried that and it hasn't worked, or if the problems are so serious that you really do need to go straight to your boss, or if your coworker is hostile and there's no way that talking to her directly will work out well for anyone, use the advice above.

4. Your boss expects you to answer emails and phone calls at night and over the weekend

If your boss regularly fills your evenings and weekends with non-urgent work calls and emails, you might conclude that she expects you to be available then. However, it's possible that by setting some boundaries, you can effectively push back on your boss's expectations and recover that time for yourself. In pushing back, it's also possible that you'll discover that her expectations aren't, in fact, flexible. But an awful lot of the time, it can turn out that they are.

The first thing to do is to make sure you're interpreting your boss's expectations correctly. If you receive an email at night or on the weekend, there's a very good chance that your boss doesn't actually expect you to reply until the next business day. She might be working and sending you questions as they come up, but not expecting you to deal with them until you're back at work. So the very first step here is to ask about that, by saying something like:

- *"I'm assuming that it's fine for me to wait to reply to emails sent at night or over the weekend until I'm back at work, unless something is obviously urgent. Let me know if that's not the case!"*

But if your boss makes it clear that she does indeed expect evening or weekend responses (and you're not in a field like, say, rock star crisis management where that's par for the course), try saying something like this:

- *"It's really important to me to have time to disconnect and recharge outside of work. Sometimes that means turning off my phone or not checking email for the weekend. I'll of course put in extra hours when something is an emergency, but my preference would be to respond to non-urgent things when I'm back at work. Could we try that for a while and see how it goes?"*

If the answer is a firm no, then at that point you'd need to decide if you want the job knowing that these are the terms. But very often when you have this conversation, you'll discover that there's more flexibility than you might have thought.

Four Phrases to Use
When You Talk to Your Boss

Keep these useful phrases in your pocket to use when talking to your boss:

1. **"I of course can do it that way, but I want to flag that X could potentially be a problem if we do."** If you think that something your manager is asking you to do is a bad idea, this is a way to say so without seeming argumentative. You're clearly saying that you'll do what he has asked, but you're also offering another perspective that he might find helpful.

2. **"I realized that I wasn't totally sure what you meant when you said X earlier."** If your manager says something that leaves you confused or alarmed, ask about it! Even if you didn't think to bring it up in the moment, it's okay to ask about it later. In fact, most managers would want you to, so that they're able to clarify what they meant.

3. **"Thanks for telling me that—it's really useful to hear."** If you're cheerful and openly appreciative when your manager gives you feedback, she'll be more inclined to continue doing it. And she'll probably think of you as incredibly easy to work with, too.

4. **"Can I repeat back my understanding of what you just told me to make sure I've got it right?"** This is a good question to ask if your boss doesn't always think to mention crucial details until you're halfway through an assignment or if you don't always leave conversations with the same understanding. Giving a brief summary of what you're taking away from the conversation can help you both spot places where you might not be on the same page.

5. You don't have enough work

I get a surprising number of letters from people who are worried because they have hardly anything to do at work. If you're super-busy, that might sound like a lovely situation to be in, but in reality it can be mind-numbingly boring and anxiety-producing (what will it mean for your job security if your boss notices that you're not doing very much?).

If you don't have much work *and* you're relatively new to the job (say, six months or less), the issue might be that your boss hasn't figured out yet how much you can handle or is being too slow in training you on new projects. If that's the case, try saying something like this:

- *"I wanted to talk with you about my workload. I'm finding that I'm able to finish everything on my plate fairly quickly, and I'd love to take on more. Are there other projects that I could work on?"*

If you're not so new to the job, you can use that same language—but since you've been around longer, you're also better positioned to propose things you could work on. In that case, you could consider drawing up a list of projects that you'd like to be involved with and that you think would be useful to your organization. Show your boss the list and say:

- *"I'm finding that I'm getting all my work done with time to spare, and I'd like to take on more. Would you be okay with my working on some or all of the projects on this list?"*

If none of these approaches help and you're still fielding regular boredom, another option is to just ask your manager if it's okay for you to use slow periods to work on other things. Ideally these would be at least nominally work-related, such as developing a skill or reading industry news, since that's pretty easy to say yes to (and your manager won't have to worry about the optics for anyone who walks by and sees you doing those things). You can be pretty direct about that:

- *"When I'm in a slower period with work, is it okay for me to read management blogs / do some Java tutorials / catch up on professional journals?"*

These are better options than spending a ton of time on social media or playing games on your phone, and most managers will be appreciative that you asked.

6. You want to take on more responsibility

If you're confident that you've proved yourself in your current role and you want to take on more responsibility, you'll have the best shot at success if you're specific about what you'd like to take on. Do you want to get more management experience? Overhaul your organization's social media presence? Set up a company-wide community volunteering program? Whatever it is, think through the details of how that would work (and how you'd integrate it with your existing responsibilities) and then say something like this:

- *"I'm really interested in hiring work, and I wondered if you'd be open to letting me take more of a role in the department's hiring. I'd be excited to screen résumés or do initial phone interviews for our junior positions, and now that we've automated our monthly reporting, I think I'd have enough time to take it on. Is that something we could experiment with?"*

- *"While you were out last month, I led two new employee trainings and really enjoyed presenting and answering questions. I'd love to move more in that direction with my work. Would you be open to letting me do more of that, maybe starting with covering for you when you're busy?"*

If your boss says no, don't be shy about asking whether there's a way to work toward it in the future. For example:

- *"Since this is an area I'm really interested in, I'd love your advice on what I can work on in the coming months to lay the groundwork for moving in that direction in the future."*

How to tell your manager "I know what I'm doing"

A reader writes:

I have been at my position for over a year and a half. I work in a college administrative office. We offer small business counseling for free twice a month. And twice a month, the woman in charge of the program tells me how to process the clients needing counseling. It's simple things—copy this, check off the list, etc. I feel like she is insulting my intelligence by constantly telling me how to do these simple tasks.

She is older (60s/70s) and I'm young (25). How do I kindly say to her "I know what I'm doing"? I feel like I'm being treated like a child.

Say this: "I've noticed you go over this with me each time we do this, and it makes me wonder—have I been making mistakes or otherwise not doing this correctly?" Don't say it in a snotty tone; say it in a tone of genuine concern.

That might be enough to make the point to her that you've got it and don't need it repeated each time. Or alternately, you might find out that she has some concern that you weren't aware of and that she's not addressing head-on.

And in general, that's always the right approach to take with this kind of thing—if someone is treating you in a way that seems condescending or untrusting or inappropriately micromanagey, express genuine concern about what might be causing it. It's a reasonably direct but nonaggressive way into a conversation about what's going on.

But if that doesn't work with her, then you can try, "I really do know the process well at this point, and I hate to have you spend your time reviewing it with me so often. Could I take it from here and check in with you if I run into questions?"

And if *that* doesn't work . . . well, at that point you accept that she's oddly neurotic about this program and you're going to be receiving very basic instructions about it twice a month.

7. You believe you have unreasonable deadlines

If you find yourself facing deadlines that seem unreasonable, talk to your boss! It's possible that by talking it through, you'll discover that a deadline isn't as firm as it originally seemed, or your boss will be more open to pushing it back once he hears it's causing problems. Or you might find that it's fine to use shortcuts that you had assumed wouldn't be okay, or that it's really only a particular piece of the project that has to be ready on time.

The best way to initiate this conversation is to explain what you *can* do and offer some options for how to proceed. For example:

- *"I can have a full mock-up in three days, but I won't have time to fully test it by then. I could finish the testing by Monday, though. Would that work?"*

- *"To get this done by Thursday, I'd need to push everything else back, which means that I wouldn't finish up X and Y until next week. Would that be okay?"*

But what if your manager tells you no, you need to stick to the original deadline with no modifications and you can't push any of your other work back? If you genuinely don't believe you can meet the deadline, say this:

- *"I hear you on how important it is to get it done by then. I'll do everything I can to make it happen, but I want to be transparent with you that I'm concerned that factors X and Y mean that it's going to take longer. Let me really push on it over the next twenty-four hours and then update you once I see where I am."*

8. Your workload is too heavy

Often when people are overwhelmed by their workload, they assume their managers are aware of how much is on their plate. But in reality, no one pays as much attention to your workload as you do. Many managers assume that you'll speak up if it gets to be too much—and that if you're not saying anything, everything must be fine.

I once coaxed an admission out of an employee—with great effort, because he did not want to share this—that the team he managed had been overloaded with projects for months (and had a terrible backlog of overdue work). He hadn't spoken up about it because he figured that if we kept sending them new projects, they must be expected to some-how handle it all. I was horrified, and within a week, we had significantly pared back his team's workload. And he hadn't even been planning to mention it until I dragged it out of him!

So. Talk to your manager. Ideally you should suggest a few different options to adjust your workload, like this:

- *"I can do A and B, but not C. Or, if C is really important, I could move A off my plate to make room for it. Or I could act as an adviser to Lavinia if she took on C, but I can't do C myself if I'm also doing A and B."*

A decent manager, upon hearing this, will talk through options with you. But if your boss resists making any trade-offs, say this:

- *"I hear you that we want to get it all done, but since realistically I don't have time to juggle all of it, I want to make sure that I'm making the right choices about priorities and focusing on the most important things. Otherwise I worry that since I can't do it all, the things that don't get done may be the wrong things."*

And if you're so overwhelmed that you can't even begin to figure out options to propose to your manager, you can still say something. In that case, just be honest:

- *"I'm finding that I've taken on way too much, and the stress of trying to juggle it all is exhausting me. I'm worried it will impact my work at some point. Can we take a look at my workload and figure out how to make it more manageable?"*

9. You're going to miss a deadline

If you think you're in danger of missing a deadline, the most important thing you can do is to speak up as soon as you realize it. Don't wait until right before the deadline, and definitely don't wait until the deadline has passed. The less advance notice you give your boss, the harder the message will be to deliver—because the closer it is to the deadline, the fewer options she's likely to have. If she has plenty of advance notice, she can bring in extra help, move other priorities around, and give a heads-up to anyone else who's going to be affected. Waiting until the last minute takes away most of those options.

As soon as you realize your deadline is in jeopardy, say something like this:

- *"I'm concerned that I might not be able to meet the deadline for the piece on dinosaur aficionados. I've just finished the research and am about to start the draft, but it's due at the end of the week and I also have that all-day strategy meeting tomorrow and the follow-up that will come out of that."*

Then, if possible, suggest options:

- *"I could definitely have it done by next Tuesday, but that's two days later than we'd discussed. Or I could skip tomorrow's meeting, although I know that's not ideal. What do you think makes sense?"*

10. You missed a deadline

If you didn't give your manager advance warning and now you've missed a deadline, what do you do?

This is a pretty serious mistake, so you want to make it clear that you recognize that. Your manager is going to worry not just about the late project itself, but also whether he can rely on you in the future—so it's important to talk about what you're going to do differently in the future so it doesn't happen again. For example:

- *"I'm so sorry that I'm turning this in late. I thought I was going to be able to get it done on time, but I didn't estimate correctly how long it would take to finish. I should have communicated with you earlier, and I'll make sure that I do in the future. I'm also going to carve out more time for this type of project from now on, so that I'll have a buffer if something takes longer than I anticipated."*

11. Asking for feedback

While being left in peace to do your work with no criticism might sound like a pretty good deal, in reality it can be a very *bad* deal. At a minimum, not getting feedback means that you won't know about any problems with your work or ways that you could do a better job. That can affect what you do or don't accomplish in your job, as well as the kind of reputation you build with other people. At worst, it can mean that your manager has serious concerns about your work that you don't know about until it's too late to fix them.

So trust me, as long as you have a halfway decent manager, you want feedback. (In fact, even if you *don't* have a halfway decent manager, it's still useful for you to know what she thinks of your work. Being blindsided by the discovery that your manager is unhappy with you is never a good thing.)

But what if your manager doesn't give you much feedback? Weirdly, a lot of managers don't, even though it's a key part of their job. But if you go out of your way to ask for feedback about your work, many managers will be glad to give it.

Say it this way:

- *"I really value feedback about my work and what I could do better. Would you be willing to share your thoughts on how things are going overall and on ways that I could be more effective?"*

If the response you get is vague or unhelpful ("Everything's fine!"), try asking this instead:

- *"If I were going to pick one thing to work on improving, what would you like to see me focus on?"*

If your manager struggles to give you big-picture job performance feedback, see if you can get feedback on individual pieces of work instead. Ask to debrief on a recent project or drill down into specific elements of what you do. For example:

- *"Could we talk through how this campaign went and what we could have done differently to get better results?"*

- *"I'm not sure the framework I'm using is the most effective one. Could I run through it for you and get your input on how to strengthen it?"*

- *"Can I tell you how I'm planning to approach tomorrow's meeting with the school board and see what you think?"*

"I just wanted to share that, one year into my first full-time job post-graduation, I finally got up the courage to ask a fairly uncommunicative boss for feedback, and it's worked out so far! The feedback was more negative than I expected, so at first I was devastated, but then I read your post on receiving criticism gracefully and swallowed my pride and asked for specifics . . . and now not only do I feel better about my job because I know what I need to improve instead of only guessing and feeling alternately great and terrible at my job, but my bosses are actually being a lot nicer to me! Having this feedback really helped because some of the things I was worried about apparently weren't even on the radar—and I could make plans on what I needed to improve! And I figure things can only go up from here."

—Letter from a reader

12. Asking to hear feedback more consistently/promptly, not after it's festered

Getting regular feedback from your boss is a good thing, especially because it *sucks* to find out that something has been a problem for months and months but you're just hearing about it now. Managers who don't give regular feedback will often let problems fester until they're so big that the conversation can no longer be avoided, at which point things are often harder to fix.

If this happens to you, ask to hear feedback more consistently or promptly in the future! You don't want to be confrontational about it, of course, but you can say something like this:

- *"I really appreciate knowing that this has been a problem. Could I ask you to talk to me earlier if there are problems in the future? I'd be really grateful to know when you have concerns so that I can hear the feedback and start working on it right away."*

This is effective in part because the reason managers stall on giving critical feedback is often that they're reluctant to upset people or to have an awkward conversation. If you make it clear that you *want* that conversation to take place, it can help break down their hesitation.

13. You disagree with your manager's feedback

Ultimately, it's your manager's call to decide how to assess your work. But sometimes you might have additional information that might change his mind, or you might feel strongly that there's another perspective worth considering.

When that happens, a good framework is "I definitely see what you're saying. I was thinking of it more like X—is that not right?"

For example, if your boss is concerned that you're not always getting back to coworkers immediately, but your understanding was that he wanted you prioritizing customer calls, you could say:

- *"I definitely see what you're saying. I was thinking that I should always prioritize calls from customers over anything else, and sometimes that means a delay in responding internally. Is that not the right way to approach it?"*

The key point here is not to argue with your manager's viewpoint; you're simply sharing yours and asking with genuine openness whether you should be looking at the situation differently. It's possible he'll say yes, you should be (or that there's more nuance to the situation than you realized), but it's also possible that hearing your perspective will change your boss's own assessment.

(Of course, you don't want to push back every single time you get feedback. If that's happening, it's a sign that you and your manager may have irreconcilable differences in how you each see your work and you may need to decide whether the job and the manager are the right ones for you.)

14. Your manager is a bottleneck in your work

If your manager is creating a bottleneck in your workflow—delaying work from moving forward because of her lag in giving input or approval—she may not be aware that she's causing a problem.

Start by pointing out the problem and asking if there's something that you can do differently on your end to move things forward more quickly. For example:

- *"I know that you get a ton of work coming at you for review. Is there anything I can do differently that would help you get back to me more quickly? I've almost missed a few deadlines recently because things got held up in editing and approval. Would it be easier on your end if I brought printouts to our meetings so you could look at them on the spot? Or are there things I could just move forward with on my own?"*

Note that the approach here isn't just a complaint that your boss isn't turning things around quickly enough. It's "Help me figure out if there's something I can do on my end that would create a better system for both of us."

You can also try heading off the problem when you first send work over, by saying something like:

- *"In order to meet the printer deadline on this, I need your edits no later than Tuesday."*

And then if you haven't heard anything by Monday:

- *"I wanted to remind you that I need your edits on this by tomorrow in order not to miss the printer deadline."*

If you do both of these things and don't see much improvement, then it might be that your boss really does just have more pressing demands that she needs to prioritize. If that's the case, then you'd want to shift the conversation to something like this:

- *"I know that you're squeezing in your review of this stuff around a zillion other priorities and that you can't always turn them around as quickly as you'd like. Should we just accept that the reality is that sometimes these things will be delayed, and there's not much we can do about it?"*

Sometimes that conversation can help both of you manage your expectations . . . and can take some of the pressure off you to figure out how to get something from her that she isn't realistically able to give you.

15. Your boss is always late to meetings

It can be frustrating as hell if you set aside time to meet with your boss, possibly cutting other meetings or projects short, and then wait . . . and wait. It can feel like your boss is being inconsiderate or disrespectful of your time. Sometimes that's true—but in many cases your boss may be juggling competing demands or unexpected last-minute issues as best he can. Sometimes just keeping that in mind can make it easier to deal with when it happens.

That said, if it's happening constantly, it might make sense to say something like this:

- *"I know you're busy and often get pulled into other things that overlap with our meeting times. Is there a time that would be better to schedule them, like earlier in the day before interruptions come up, or on a slower day of the week?"*

- *"What's the best thing for me to do when you end up getting pulled away to something else when we're scheduled to meet? Do you want me to try to find you when that happens, or wait ten minutes and then email you to reschedule?"*

If these aren't one-on-one meetings and there's a whole group of you gathered to wait for him, consider saying something like:

- *"I know you're really busy and often get pulled into other things right before our meeting times. Is it okay if the rest of us go ahead and start, and then you'll join us when you can?"*

16. Your manager keeps canceling meetings

As with a boss who's always late to meetings, a boss who constantly cancels your meetings may have legitimate reasons for doing so. But that doesn't mean it doesn't have an impact on you, and it's okay for you to bring it up. In fact, your boss may appreciate your bringing it up, because she may not realize that it's causing problems for you. (If that seems ridiculous to you, consider that people complain incessantly about having to attend meetings. Your boss may really not think you mind when yours get canceled.)

So the thing to do is to tell her very clearly that you'd like to find a way to make your meetings happen. Say something like this:

- *"I know you're really busy and things often get in the way of our meetings, but it's important to me to have some regular time with you to discuss projects and get your input. Is there a different time we could schedule for, one that's less likely to get interrupted? Or could we try shorter or even impromptu meetings whenever you have a chance to grab me?"*

And don't discount that last suggestion! I once had a boss with a ridiculously busy schedule who was notorious for canceling meetings. I really needed time with him in order to move my projects forward, so I told him that I'd happily tag along with him whenever he'd let me and that I didn't care *where* we had our meetings. He took me up on it—twice I ended up meeting with him in a hair salon while he had his hair cut—and I got what I needed.

17. Your boss doesn't answer your emails

If emailing your boss feels no more effective than throwing a message in a bottle into the ocean, it could be your boss . . . or it could be the way you're writing your emails.

Since it's easier to change the way you're writing your emails, tackle it from that end first. Make sure that your messages are as brief as possible, start with the upshot (no burying a question in multiple paragraphs of context!), and have super-clear subject lines ("Can I confirm June 10 as the gala date?" is a lot clearer than "Gala date"). And make it easy for your boss to reply quickly, by proposing solutions, asking yes/no questions, and otherwise making it simple for him to write back things like "Yes, sounds good" or "Let's do option 2."

But if you're doing all that and still not getting responses, then talk to your boss and ask if there's a better way to get what you need:

- *"I tend to use email when I need things from you, figuring that it's easier for you to respond when it's convenient for you and that you'll have all the info you need in front of you. But I've been having trouble getting answers that way, and I wonder if you'd rather I do something differently when I have questions or need quick input."*

You might hear that your manager would prefer that you come talk to him in person or call him (which will be annoying if you're an email person, but is still his prerogative). Or you might hear that he wants you to follow up with him when you don't hear back. (If he says this, believe him and start doing it, even if you feel awkward about it.)

My manager is excluding me from important conversations

A reader writes:

I need to talk with my manager about why I continue to get excluded from strategic conversations when my teammates are included.

My colleague, who is just a bit more senior than me, has mentioned on more than one occasion conversations she has had with our manager about overall strategic goals for the team or the organization. Every time, I am left wondering: Wait . . . When did this conversation happen? Why wasn't I invited?

I am starting to worry that there is something larger at play here. Does my boss not like me or think I do good work? I think she likes me quite a bit. I've independently led several projects that have generated so much positive publicity for the organization and for her as my supervisor. When I needed a recommendation letter, she told me she would be thrilled to write one and only had glowing things to say about my work. Likewise, when I had my midyear performance review, it was truly the best I'd had.

I would like to approach her about my feeling that I am not getting invited to important conversations. I want to know why that is, so that if it is an impression I am giving, I can stop it immediately. Your thoughts?

Talk to her! Say something like this: "Penelope often mentions to me that she's been talking with you about our team's strategic goals or the organization's long-term vision, and I'd love to be included in conversations like that. I know those conversations often happen spontaneously, but when there are opportunities to loop me in and you think it makes sense, I'd really like to be included."

And if it fits in with the conversation, you can also ask, "Are there things I could do differently that would lead me to being more involved in those types of discussions?"

Which leads me to this: This might be less about something you're doing wrong and more about something that your coworker is doing right. If she's initiating strategic conversations with your manager and volunteering for projects, she might simply be making herself visible in a way that you're not. In other words, it might not be that your manager is deliberately leaving you out, but rather that your coworker is putting herself in. If that's the case, you might look for ways you can do that as well.

In fact, if you have a good relationship with your coworker, you could ask her about that. Say something like, "I've noticed you and Emma often talk about things like this. I'd love to have those types of conversations with her too, but for some reason I don't seem to. Do you have any insight into how you've been able to make that happen, so that I can figure out what I can do on my end?" You might hear something in response that's as simple as, "Oh, I just ask."

18. Your manager yells at you

Hopefully you'll go your whole career without getting yelled at by a manager. Yelling is unprofessional and abusive, and good managers don't do it.

But if you do have a boss who yells, the first thing to know is that you shouldn't take it personally. Yelling is about the yeller, not about you.

Second, it's entirely reasonable to ask your boss not to speak to you that way. You've signed on to do a job, not to be verbally abused, and it's okay to say, "Hey, I'm not okay with this."

Because yellers tend to have needy egos, it can help to start the conversation by saying something positive—something that will lay down a foundation of "I like you and I want to make this work." From there, ask directly for the yelling to stop. For example:

- *"I really like my job here and I generally enjoy working for you. But I have a lot of trouble hearing your feedback when you yell at me. It's not that I don't want feedback on my work—I do, and I value it. But I don't want to be yelled at."*

Yellers are intimidating, so this might feel a little nerve-racking to say. But a lot of yellers are embarrassed after their outbursts and know it's not really okay, and they'll respect a direct request to cut it out. (In fact, addressing it directly and firmly will often increase the respect that yellers have for you.)

19. Your boss micromanages you

If your boss seems unable to trust you to do your work without constant oversight and guidance, you're probably pretty frustrated.

It's helpful to realize that most managers who micromanage do it for one of two reasons: (1) You've given them reason to, because you've been dropping the ball, forgetting details, or producing work that isn't the quality it needs to be, or (2) They lack the management skills to oversee and guide your work without getting inappropriately involved.

If your situation falls into the first category—you're getting micromanaged because you haven't been performing well—the best thing you can do is focus on demonstrating a sustained track record of better performance. (That's a nicer way of saying "You need to get your act together.")

But if it's the second category—your manager micromanages because she doesn't seem to know how to do things differently—you're justified in asking for more autonomy. The key here is to propose alternate ways of ensuring she stays in the loop. For example:

- *"I'm hoping we can talk about how we structure my projects. I've noticed that you like me to check in with you a lot as I'm working, sometimes every day and often at each stage of a project, and that you'll sometimes take the work back over after assigning it to me. If you have concerns about my work that are leading you to manage me this way, I very much want to know, so that I can work on those things. But if you don't have concerns, and you agree that I've consistently managed my work well, then I wonder if we can revisit the level of oversight. Specifically, I want to propose that I send you a weekly overview of where all my key proj-*

ects stand and that we have a weekly check-in to make sure we're aligned on how work is moving forward. Aside from that meeting, I'd like to be able to move ahead with projects independently, unless there's some specific problem we need to address. Would you be willing to try that for the next month and see how it goes?"

You might also propose specific things you'd like to have the authority to run with on your own. For instance:

- *"I've built up a good track record of managing routine problems that arise with the classes I'm teaching. Could we say I'll move forward on those without checking in with you, unless something unusual arises or there's something a student is especially concerned about?"*

20. You want to say no to a new job duty

If you're asked to take on something new that you really don't want to do, whether or not to push back depends on a few different factors: how reasonable it is to expect the person in your role to take on this work, the rest of your workload (if you're swamped with other things, it's easier to say no than if you have time on your hands), and your standing with your employer (how valued you are and how much goodwill you have built up).

If those factors seem in your favor, try speaking up. Depending on the circumstances, here are a few different ways to approach it:

- *"I'm concerned about fitting this in with the rest of my workload. My plate is pretty full with X, Y, and Z, and I'm not sure it's feasible to add this on top of it."*

- *"I'm honestly not sure I'd be the best person for this. It requires skills in C and D, which frankly aren't my strong suits. Would you be open to seeing if someone else is interested in taking this on, and having me continue to focus on A and B, which I think I'm doing well?"*

- *"I want to be up-front with you that one of the reasons I took this job over others was that it didn't involve doing X. I'm of course willing to help out in a pinch, but I'd be concerned about making this a permanent part of my responsibilities, since it's so far afield from what I want to be doing."*

- *"This is a pretty substantial increase in my responsibilities—and stress! If you're envisioning it being a permanent addition to my role, could we revisit my title and compensation so that they reflect this?"*

Ultimately, your manager does have the ability to say, "Sorry, this is just part of the job now." So in having this conversation, you want your tone to reflect that understanding. Your tone should signal "I'm hoping we might be able to handle this differently," not "I will not do what you're asking."

If it does turn out that your boss won't budge, then at that point you'll need to decide if you still want the job under these new conditions . . . but try seeing if there's any flexibility first.

Can I decline additional duties if I don't get a raise or promotion?

A reader writes:

Can and how do I professionally decline additional duties/ responsibilities unless I receive a pay raise or promotion?

Background: I've been in the same position for almost four years. I've been promised multiple pay raises (including to bring me up to industry standard), which have never happened "for budgetary reasons."

In the last seven months, our management team has dwindled from four people running three departments and reporting to my boss to two, and one of them has just put in his notice. My boss is already telling him to give me all of his tool access so I can do his job as well but has never spoken to me about it. I am overwhelmed and underpaid. I am not willing to take on this stress unless I receive a pay raise and promotion. How can I decline the additional responsibilities unless I receive a pay raise and promotion, without being fired for insubordination?

Well, if you simply say, "No, pay me more or I won't do that," you're likely to hear "Sorry, but this is part of the job now" . . . and the subtext will be "Take it or leave it."

But there's a better way to go about this—not one that's guaranteed to work, but one that's certainly a reasonable and professional way to proceed.

Meet with your boss and say something like this: "I'm concerned about the increasing workload that I'm being asked to handle. Our management team has gone from four people to two, and is about to go to one, and I'm picking up most of the work that used to be handled by other people. My plate is more than full at this point, and it's a real challenge to juggle everything I'm now responsible for. I can help out on a short-term basis, but this has been the case for months and looks like it will continue and maybe even get worse. It's a significant amount of stress and responsibility. I'm willing to continue helping out, but I want to revisit my title and my compensation. It's not feasible for me to continue with this increased workload at my current level of pay—which is the same pay level I've been at for four years, even though I've been told I'd receive raises in the past, and then never have. What can we do to get my pay and title up to something that reflects the work I'm doing?"

And be prepared to be asked what salary you want, which means researching and thinking this through beforehand so that you don't undercut yourself or ask for more than is realistic.

From there, listen to what your boss says. If he agrees, then great, problem solved . . . although make sure that the raise really happens this time, by following up your conversation with an email summarizing your agreement and setting a date for the raise to be effective, and then circling back immediately if you don't see the raise by the time you're supposed to.

But if he hems and haws, say this: "I understand that you can't decide this on the spot, but I'm serious about figuring out how to proceed fairly quickly, since this has been going on for a while now. Can I follow up with you in a week?"

If you're told that your requests can't be granted and

the work just has to be done, then there's your answer. Your company is not going to give you a raise or a promotion, and they're not going to change your workload. At that point, you'd need to decide if you want the job as it's being offered (this salary, this title, this workload) or if you'd rather look for work elsewhere. Meanwhile, though, as long as you stay, you probably do need to do the work you're being assigned . . . or at least, you can't flatly refuse it.

However—and this is important—you can and should say things like, "I can do X, Y, and Z in forty hours a week" (or forty-five, or whatever the norm is in your industry), "which means that A, B, and C will be on the back burner until I have time to get to them, which may not be for a while." That's a matter of prioritizing your responsibilities—it's different from saying, "No, I refuse to accept A, B, and C altogether."

Meanwhile, you can certainly be looking for another job . . . and once you find one, leave and explain why.

21. You need more training

In a lot of jobs, it's not uncommon to be expected to figure out how to do things on your own. But if you're at a point where you've done all you can and you don't think you can succeed without additional training, speak up! Your manager may not realize that you need help unless you tell him—and it's far better to speak up now than down the road when your lack of training has caused problems.

If possible, try to figure out what training you need so that you can approach your boss with a specific proposal, whether it's a course, one-on-one time with someone who has the skill you need to develop, or something else:

- *"I'm finding that I don't have as strong a background in X as I think I need in order to do Y successfully. Would you be open to sending me to this course I've found that looks like it will cover all the fundamentals?"*

Or, if what you really need training in is specific to your company, try wording like this:

- *"I'm realizing that I could use better grounding in how we work with community leaders and how to handle some of the sensitive questions that come up. Could we schedule an hour this week and an hour next week to go over some of the situations I've been running into and talk through how I should be handling them?"*

22. Your manager doesn't lay out clear expectations

If you're lucky, your boss is pretty good at telling you what she expects from you. But a lot of managers are surprisingly bad at this and may leave you in the dark about what a project should look like when done well, or even what it looks like to perform your role well overall.

If you find yourself with a boss who doesn't set clear expectations, it's crucial to find ways to draw those expectations out of her. Otherwise you can end up prioritizing the wrong things, approaching projects in the totally wrong way, and neglecting major pieces of the work that you'll be evaluated on.

To be clear, it shouldn't *have* to be your job to hunt these things down, but if the reality is that that's the only way to get clear expectations out of your manager, it's in your best interests to do it.

If your boss tends to assign you work without being clear about what she really wants and you discover once you turn it in that she was envisioning something totally different from what you produced, try speaking up when she's first delegating an assignment to you:

- *"To make sure I go in the right direction with this, could we talk about how you're envisioning the final product? Are there particular elements that I should make sure to include, or any background I should know? And how should I prioritize this relative to other projects?"*

If your boss is fuzzy about the overall expectations for your *role*—not just specific projects—that's a bigger-picture conversation:

- *"I'm hoping we can talk about the big-picture expectations for my role. Sometimes you've asked me to focus on X and not to worry much about Y or Z. But at other times, Y and Z have ended up becoming bigger focuses. I want to make sure that I'm aligned with you on how I should be spending my time and how my performance is being measured, so that I'm spending my energy in the right places. Could we talk through some of the conflicting priorities I've encountered in my role and hopefully nail down some overall principles for the big areas I should be focusing on?"*

How to disagree with your boss

Good managers want to hear perspectives that are different from their own, because they want to ensure they're getting to the best solution. But of course, when you disagree with your boss, you want to do it respectfully, not adversarially.

Here are some good ways to disagree without being confrontational:

• "If we went in that direction, I'd worry about X."

• "My take was a little different. I thought X."

• "Is it worth considering X?"

Be sure to ground your argument in what makes sense for the organization, and take the time to explain the assumptions underlying your argument. (Those assumptions might not be as clear as you think they are!)

Ultimately, of course, it's your boss's prerogative to make the final call. If you share your input and she's not convinced, sometimes you can try a second time if there's new information to add (for example, "In case it influences your thinking, one additional thing to consider is . . ."), but after that you generally need to accept that she's heard you out and made a different decision.

23. Your boss contradicts himself on priorities or work instructions

Worse than a boss with fuzzy expectations is one with very clear expectations one day and a completely different set the next day—and who expects you to read his mind.

If your boss tends to change his mind about a project without telling you, the first thing to do is to make a point of checking in more often. For example, if you're working on a monthlong project, make sure you're not just talking about it once at the start and then again when you turn it in four weeks later. Check in while you're working on the project by saying something like:

- *"Things are moving along with the X project. I'm still working under the assumption that we should be doing Y and Z with it. Does that still sound right, or should I make any adjustments?"*

You can also try naming the issue and asking for advice on how to navigate it:

- *"I've noticed that the details of projects or their priority levels can change pretty quickly, and I don't always know when that has happened. As a result, I'm sometimes moving forward on work in a way that's different from what you want, but neither of us realizes it until later in the process. Is there a way for us to touch base more quickly when something changes, so that you're getting what you need from me and I'm not spending time on something when the project needs have changed?"*

Note that you're not blaming your boss; you're just calmly observing that this sometimes happens and are seeking a solution to help you do your job well. Your focus isn't on your frustration about the frequent changes, but on figuring out how to navigate those changes.

There are also times when you might have work-related reasons (not just frustration) for asking your boss to commit to a path and stop changing his mind. In that case, you could say something like this:

- *"I know this kind of thing can end up changing a few times before we settle on a final plan. I'm going to be out of the office after Thursday, so it would be really tough to make any changes after today. Can we firmly commit to this plan since there's such a small window of time for getting it moving?"*

And if your boss ever seems to blame you for not reading his mind and knowing that he changed his opinion on something, try calmly explaining where you're coming from:

- *"I'll of course be happy to do it the new way, but I want to make sure you know that I wasn't ignoring your instructions earlier. When we talked about this last week, you'd okayed doing X, so I was working from that assumption. Now that I know you want me to do Y instead, I will definitely make that adjustment. I just want to make sure you know why I was doing X to begin with."*

24. Your boss is making offensive jokes

If your boss has a habit of making offensive—racist, sexist, homophobic, sexual, or otherwise inappropriate—jokes, it can be hard to figure out how to respond. After all, this is your boss, and most people don't feel super-comfortable calling out someone with authority over them for being offensive. But there's usually more leeway for speaking up than you might think.

Knowing exactly how to handle it depends on your boss, your relationship, and your sense of the situation, but here are some options:

- Ignore it—but pointedly. In some cases, if you pause, look taken aback, and then pointedly resume the conversation that was taking place before the joke was made, you'll get your message across without having to say anything.

- Use the "I don't get it" strategy, which is handy for dealing with bigoted jokes from anyone: *I don't get what you mean. Can you explain it?* Most people will quickly back off rather than spell out whatever bigotry was the foundation of the "joke"—and you'll signal that you're not a receptive audience in the future.

You can also call it out directly:

- *"I really don't like that kind of joke."* If you think it will go over better, you can add some face-saving language: *"I know you're just kidding, but I really don't like that kind of joke."*

- *"You're normally so respectful, and I figured you'd want to know that comment didn't land the way you probably intended."*

- *"I don't see that as funny."*

- *"Eeeww, please don't say things like that around me."*

- *"I wanted to talk to you about the joke you made earlier. I know you didn't mean to be offensive, but it made me uncomfortable because it was at the expense of women / people of color / gay people."*

My boss thinks he is a Mayan shaman

A reader writes:
I took a job at a nonprofit as an economic researcher about seven months ago. Overall, I love my job and what I get to do and helping people, but there is one major issue: My boss, who is the founder and head of the organization, thinks he is a Mayan shaman. I am not joking.

He spends crazy amounts of money to fund his "spiritual projects" and recently has been telling me to do projects like comparing chakra colors in different cultures and staring at a candle to find a sacred angle. Seriously. I've been able to handle it just fine until now. He is getting crazier by the day and I don't know how to handle it anymore because if I tell him anything, he will say the "darkness has possessed me" and then be uncommunicative when I need information.

What can I do? Is there anything? I don't want to quit my job but this is getting out of hand. He sends texts to us in the middle of the night with his "visions" and when one of our employees was pregnant he would *call it "the Christ Child" and say that one quarter of the DNA must be his. I swear this is not a fake situation or question.*

Shamans have to have day jobs, I guess.

And he's welcome to believe he's a shaman. Who knows, maybe he is. But the problem here is that he's letting his spiritual beliefs interfere with work.

But I doubt there's a lot you can do here. This is your boss, the head of the organization, and ultimately he's calling the shots. If you really want to try to get this addressed, you have two options: Talk to him directly or talk to the board of directors.

If you talk to him directly, I'd say something like this: "Percival, I respect your religious beliefs, but I'm not comfortable discussing religion at work or being given religious assignments to work on. I was hired to do economic research and our organization isn't religious in nature. Is there a way for us to work well together without bringing religion into it?" Ideally, you'd do this with a group of coworkers who feel the same way you do rather than on your own; it's harder to ignore a group of employees than one lone voice, but either way, it's a reasonable thing to say.

But will it work? I doubt it. This is a guy who's telling you that darkness has possessed you and claiming some sort of parentage over a quarter of an employee's baby. In other words, he's probably not open to reasoned conversation on these topics.

So that leaves you with the second option: Talk to the board. The board is this guy's boss and would presumably want to know that the head of the organization is using its resources to find sacred candle angles and

freezing out employees when he thinks they're possessed.

But, that said . . . unless you care passionately about
this organization and want to take an active role in getting this situation straightened out, your best bet might
be to leave. This situation isn't likely to change overnight,
there's likely to be some tension if you go to the board,
and—maybe most important—do you really trust this
guy's leadership, even if he cools it with the shaman
talk? I mean, let's say that the board puts a stop to all the
behavior you've written about, and it even happens
quickly—you're still going to be working at an organization led by a guy who thought all of this was reasonable
to begin with. Is that the job you want?

In light of that, it might make sense to skip all these
steps and just start working on leaving.

Or you could just embrace the whole thing and have
him influence the spirit world in your favor. That could
be useful too.

25. You have moral or ethical issues with something your boss asks you to do

From time to time, we all get asked to do things at work that
we're not super-enthused about. Most of the time, that's just
part of having a job. But when something violates your mor-
als or ethics, that's something you can speak up about: Plainly
state that you're uncomfortable, explain the potential consequences if relevant, and suggest a different way of proceeding.

For example, if your boss asks you to fudge some data, you
could say this:

- *"I really don't feel right entering data we know isn't accurate. I think we could get in real trouble if it ever came out, and it would be a huge blow to our credibility. But I think we could get the correct data by Monday. I know that's two days late, but I'd be much more comfortable explaining the delay to the board than putting incorrect data in there."*

If that doesn't work, try appealing to a higher authority, like your manager's own boss or someone else with more authority:

- *"I do know that Monday isn't ideal for you, but I'm really not comfortable using data that we can't back up. Could we loop in Leah about how to proceed?"*

If that doesn't work either, and you feel strongly enough that you're willing to take a firm stand, you could say it this way:

- *"I'm just not comfortable doing that. I wouldn't be able to feel okay about my work here. I know I'm causing some inconvenience to you, but I hope you understand how strongly I feel."*

26. Your boss wants to be your friend, but you want to preserve professional boundaries

If your boss is acting more like a close friend than a boss—sharing too much personal information, inviting you to hang out outside of work, or expecting things of you that are more appropriate for a friend—you're probably spending much of your work life feeling really uncomfortable.

Sometimes you can redirect an overly friendly boss back to the boss zone by vigilantly maintaining your own boundaries: turning down social invitations, remembering a work call you need to make when the conversation turns too personal, and so forth.

But if your cues aren't working, you'll probably have more success just being kind but straightforward about the boundaries you want. And one way to make that easier and less awkward for everyone is to frame it as your own weirdness, rather than a rejection of your boss in particular. For example:

- *"If we didn't work together, I'd love to take you up on your Renaissance Fair invitation. But I have a terrible pattern of becoming friends with my managers, and I've vowed to have better boundaries, so I am going to say no. Thanks for offering, though!"*

- *"You're so easy to talk to, and I've realized we keep getting drawn into personal conversations. I have a terrible pattern of becoming friends with my managers, and I've vowed to be better about professional boundaries—so I'm going to try heading those situations off and just wanted to explain, so that you didn't wonder why."*

My boss keeps stealing my lunch

A reader writes:

I've recently been transferred to a new department, working in a new office environment, under a new manager. His diet consists mainly of fast food and takeout.

I have crazy allergies to a bunch of foods, as well as chemicals found in most processed foods. Some are the swell-up-like-a-balloon-and-stop-breathing kind of allergy. I make most of my food at home and bring it with me to work. I'm really open about my allergies so that people understand I'm just defective, not rude. And most people get it. Except my manager.

He eats my lunch out of the staff fridge on an almost daily basis, as if the food fairy left him a gift. I resorted to packing meals that I could keep at my desk, and he started raiding my drawers when I would be in meetings or away from my desk. When I try to address the fact that he's stealing my food, he tries to butter me up by complimenting my cooking, then walks away.

Any thoughts on how I can handle this situation, especially strategies that don't have me going above him to complain to his manager? (Also, we have no HR department to turn to.)

Your boss is either incredibly rude or has some kind of eating compulsion problem. Or both.

You've got two choices:

1. **Talk to him directly.** Not in passing, not off-the-cuff, but a serious, sit-down conversation that sounds

something like this: "Jim, as you know, I have serious food allergies. When you eat the food that I brought to work with me, it means that I can't eat anything that day, since I can't replace it with just anything that happens to be accessible. So when you take my food, I literally cannot eat until I go home. Like most people, I don't do well when I'm starving. This is a medical issue for me. I need you to stop taking my food."

If he laughs it off, repeat again, "This is a medical issue for me. If you're going to continue taking my food, it will put me at risk of a medical problem. How can we solve this?"

If you're like most people, you probably don't feel 100 percent comfortable having this kind of stern conversation with your boss. But when you're dealing with someone so willing to violate normal boundaries, your best bet is often a simple, direct assertion that the behavior needs to stop. I'm not going to tell you that there's no chance of its creating tension between the two of you; it might. But you're so clearly in the right and he's so clearly in the wrong that it's also likely that he'll just feel sheepish and back off.

2. **Get a locking lunchbox.** You could even use a small locking toolbox or one of those lockboxes that people store money in. Get something that can be opened only with a key or a numerical combination.

But practical advice aside, he's going through your desk to steal your food, after you've asked him to stop. Something's not right with this dude.

27. You made a mistake at work

You're going to make a mistake at some point, because you're human and that is what we do. Believe me, I have made a ton of them myself, and when I think back to the most stellar people I've managed, they all made mistakes sometimes too.

The important thing to know is that the way you handle it can end up being more important than the mistake itself.

There's actually a pretty straightforward formula for telling your boss about a mistake:

1. **Tell your boss what happened right away.** Don't put it off because you're dreading the conversation. Delaying will make things worse, partly because it will send the message that you value your own comfort over the needs of your work.

2. **Take responsibility for what happened.** Don't make excuses, and don't be defensive. If you act like it wasn't a big deal or you aren't responsible for it, this will compound the damage because now your boss will be alarmed that you're cavalier about errors or don't take ownership of them. (In fact, the more concerned you seem, the less likely your boss is to feel that she needs to impress the severity of the mistake upon you, because you'll have shown that you already get it.)

3. **Explain briefly how the mistake happened.** This is important not only because your boss might want to know, but particularly because she'll want to know that *you* know. If you don't understand how a mistake happened, it's more likely to happen again.

4. **Explain how you plan to ensure it doesn't happen again.** In a lot of cases, your boss won't care so much about the de-

tails of your plan; she'll just want to know that you *have* a plan—that you're taking it seriously and will work to prevent similar mistakes in the future.

That might sound like this:

- *"I need to tell you about a problem with the newsletter that just went out. I realized this morning that one of the numbers in the lead article was wrong. This was my fault— I thought I'd fact-checked everything before it was finalized, but I missed this one. I've been pulled in a bunch of directions this week, and I rushed the newsletter process more than I should have. I'm drafting a correction to run by you, and I'm making a checklist to use in the future to make sure I don't skip any steps. If I'd done that this time, I don't think this would have happened. I'm really sorry about this!"*

28. Your boss asks nosy questions when you ask for time off

Ideally, when you ask for time off, your boss should simply approve it if you have the time accrued and it's not going to cause any serious work problems. But some managers respond to requests for a day off by asking what you'll be using it for. That isn't a big deal when it's something you don't mind talking about, but it can be a problem when your plans are private, such as a medical appointment that you'd rather not discuss.

Most of the time when managers do this, they're just being friendly; they don't intend to be nosy or intrusive and don't realize that they might be putting you in an awkward position. Because of that, if it happens once or twice, you're better off just resorting to vague answers like:

- *"Oh, just a medical thing I need to take care of."*

But if your boss does this all the time, you might say:

- *"I don't know if you realize that when I ask for time off, you usually ask me for details about why. I know you're just being friendly, but I wanted to mention that sometimes it might be a medical thing that I don't want to talk about, especially in front of other people, or a family situation that I don't want to discuss. Of course, if you ever have concerns about whether I'm using my leave time properly, definitely talk to me about it, but otherwise I wanted to suggest that we all have some privacy around days off."*

29. You want to apply for a position in a different department

In a lot of ways, applying for a job within your current organization is easier than applying for jobs externally; you know the culture and the key players and probably have a good sense of what they're looking for, and the decision-makers may already know you and your work.

One thing that's trickier about it, though, is that companies often require you to tell your current manager that you're interviewing for another role internally. That can be an awkward conversation, since most of us prefer not to tell our bosses this kind of thing until we've actually resigned. But if you find yourself in this situation, you can say it this way:

- *"I really enjoy the work I do for our team, but the opening in the X department interests me so much that I wouldn't forgive myself for not throwing my hat in the ring."*

- *"I'm really happy with my job here, but X is a passion of mine. I've decided to apply for the X role in the Y department, and I wanted to be up-front about it with you."*

30. You want a raise

People often think that asking for a raise needs to involve a lengthy justification of why you're worth more money. But most of the time, you don't need to do that! As long as you've been doing good work and it's been at least a year since your salary was last changed (or set initially), often you can simply say something like this:

- *"I was hoping that we could talk about my salary. It's been a year since my last raise, and I've taken on quite a few new responsibilities since then. I've taken over game testing and the intern program, and you've given me great feedback on how both of those have been going. I've been able to resolve the problems we were having with IT not prioritizing our requests, and I spent quite a few nights and weekends over the summer making sure that our campaign launch went successfully. I'm hoping that we might be able to talk about increasing my salary to recognize the additional work I've been doing."*

Note that this doesn't just say that you'd like more money, but reminds your manager of some specifics about what you've been doing well. At the same time, though, it's not an extensive laundry list of everything you've done in the last twelve months—just some highlights.

If you have a particular number in mind, you can include that, too:

- *"I'm hoping that we could raise my salary to $X."*

But that's optional; you don't need to name a specific number if you don't have one in mind.

Also! Don't just prepare what you'll say to make the request. Make sure you also prepare for what you'll say if the answer is no. You don't want to slink out dejected; you want to be ready to say something like:

- *"Can you tell me what it would take for me to earn a raise in the future, so that I know specifically what to work on?"*

A good manager should be willing to have that discussion with you.

31. Your boss keeps promising you a raise but it never comes through

Great news: Your boss has promised to get you a raise. Not-great news: That was months ago and your paycheck hasn't changed. Try saying this:

- *"When we talked about my salary a couple of months ago, you agreed my work warranted a raise and said you'd look into making that happen. Can I ask where that stands?"*

If your boss's answer is vague (like "Oh, yes, it's on my list to deal with"), then say:

- *"I'm obviously eager to move forward with that. Can I check back with you in a week or two?"*

If nothing else, this will hopefully prompt him to tell you if your timeline is way off and he's picturing something further out. It's also okay to ask:

- *"Do you have a sense of what the likely timeline is?"*

If you have this conversation a few times without any results, and it's been a substantial amount of time (like five months, not two weeks), at that point you're justified in wondering if this raise is actually going to materialize. In that case, you might say:

- *"I know we've been talking about this for a while, and it's important to me that my salary reflect my increased contributions here. Can you help me get a better sense of what needs to happen for the increase to go through and what time frame I should expect, so that my expectations aren't off?"*

Hopefully that should get you a more concrete answer from your boss. But if it doesn't . . . well, it's possible that you're getting strung along. It's not necessarily that your boss *intends* to string you along—but if it's been months of non-answers and vague promises, the intentions may not be as relevant as the actual result. At that point, you're probably better off deciding what you'll do if the raise never does show up, whether it's finding other reasons for being content with your job or thinking about looking elsewhere.

32. You find out you're earning significantly less than an equally qualified coworker

Finding out that your coworker is paid significantly more than you for doing the same work can feel like a slap in the face, even if you were happy with your salary previously.

My advice about what to do in this situation has changed over the years. I used to tell people to use this knowledge as background information for making your own raise request, but not to explicitly cite your coworker's pay. I also used to point out that there are all kinds of reasons that a coworker might be making more than you—for example, if the job market was tighter when she was hired, or she has a particular degree or skill that the company rewards, or she just negotiated her original offer better.

But there's been so much attention paid to the wage gap in recent years that I think that advice has become outdated. These days, if you find out your coworker is paid significantly more than you for the same work and you can't see an obvious reason for the discrepancy (such as that his performance is much better than yours or he deals with particularly tough casework), the climate is much more supportive of mentioning that knowledge when you ask for a raise.

In most situations, that mention should be part of a larger case for why you deserve a raise (see conversation 30 in this chapter for more on how to present that case). In addition to explaining why your contributions at work merit a higher salary, you could include a statement like this:

- *"I'm also aware that the range for this position goes up to at least $X for people doing comparable work with comparable seniority."*

That lets you cite your knowledge of the pay range for your role without naming specific coworkers.

But if a gender disparity is in play, you should call that out more explicitly. In the United States, paying men and women differently for the same work is illegal (even if it's because they negotiated differently). In that case, you might say something like this:

- *"Given the recent attention to the gender wage gap, I'm concerned about the disparity between Lucien's salary and my own. Can you help me understand why our salaries are so different even though we do the same job?"*

Depending on your boss's response, you should be prepared to also say:

- *"I'm concerned that we're violating the Equal Pay Law by paying a man and a woman so differently for the same work."* (Note that the "we" in that sentence is intentional; it makes the conversation feel more collaborative and less adversarial, which can give you a better chance at getting the outcome you want.)

If your manager asks how you know your coworker's salary, say this:

- *"I don't want to get sidetracked by that question because the real issue is the pay disparity. For the purpose of this conversation, can we address that?"*

33. Your office keeps bothering you when you're on vacation

If you can't go on vacation without being interrupted by non-urgent, non-emergency calls and emails from your office, you should speak up.

There *are* some jobs where being available when you're away is part of the deal—but in the vast majority of jobs, you should be able to get away for a week or two without being interrupted.

One of the most effective ways to head off vacation interruptions is to tell people ahead of time that you won't be available:

• *"I will not be answering my phone while I'm away. If you think you might need anything from me while I'm gone, let me know now, because I won't be reachable once I leave."*

And then, of course, stick to that—let incoming calls from your office go to voicemail and don't deal with them until you're back.

But if that's not practical in your office, then you need to address the problem head-on. In that case, you might say this to your boss:

• *"The last few times I've gone on vacation, I ended up getting work calls about things that weren't emergencies. It's important to me to be able to disconnect completely on this vacation. Can you help me make sure that people don't call me about work stuff while I'm away?"*

If your boss is the biggest perpetrator, say it this way:

- *"The last few times I've gone on vacation, I ended up getting work calls about things that weren't emergencies. It's important to me to be able to disconnect completely on this vacation. Can we go through anything that you think you might need from me while I'm away so that we can deal with most of it now and set up someone else to handle anything remaining?"*

If all else fails, consider saying that you'll be traveling somewhere without cellphone service.

I can overhear my boss's dirty conversations with his girlfriend

A reader writes:
My boss calls his girlfriend on the phone quite frequently. They have "lovey dovey" conversations. His door is always open, so everyone in the building can hear this. I find this annoying and unprofessional. But I'm new, it doesn't seem to bother anyone else, and he's not the most approachable person, so I have chosen to ignore it and try to block it out. The conversations are usually PG.

However, his most recent conversation went far beyond PG, as they were talking dirty to each other. It started as a "No, I miss you more," which led into him talking about various body parts and then devolved from there.

After I threw up a little in my mouth, I sat there in utter

shock that he would talk like that at work. Now I'm con-
cerned that this type of conversation might happen again
or, worse, escalate in its raciness. Do I continue to ignore
it since it doesn't seem to bother anyone else? I just can't
understand how a professional can think this is appropri-
ate work behavior.

Eeeewww.

Yes, this is wildly inappropriate.

Personally, I would choose to find this incredibly amus-
ing and file away stories to share with people later, but obviously not everyone is going to feel that way, and some/
many/most people might feel downright uncomfortable or
as if their work environment has been sexualized against
their will—which is an entirely reasonable way to feel.

If you had worked there longer and had decent rapport with him, I'd suggest just closing his door when
these conversations begin and/or saying to him, "Barnaby, I think I now know way too much about your relationship with Clarissa—can you close the door next
time?" . . . or "Did you know we can hear your conversations with Clarissa and some of them are uncomfortable
to overhear?" . . . or "Whoa, I feel like I'm working inside
a Cinemax movie" . . . or whatever "You are gross, cut it
out" formulation you felt comfortable with.

Even as a new person, you could certainly say something directly if this happens again, if you want to. For
example: "Barnaby, you probably don't realize that your
conversations can be heard over where I am. That normally isn't a problem, but I'm uncomfortable hearing
really personal ones, like the one you just had. Would
you mind if I close your door if I'm overhearing something like that again?"

But you're new, you don't find him approachable, and

no one else is saying anything. So if you don't want to take it on yourself, I see two other options:

1. **Say something to someone else, if an appropriate person exists.** Who this person is will vary by office. In some offices, your boss might have a no-nonsense assistant or deputy who could easily tell him to cut this out and be listened to. In others, you might have a competent HR department who could tell him to stop it. I don't know the dynamics of your office, but if there's someone who strikes you as sensible and who has some standing, you could discreetly have a word with that person. For example: "I like working with Barnaby, but he has a habit of having *really* personal conversations with his girlfriend with the door open, at least one of which has strayed into sexual territory. I don't want to cause awkwardness with him, especially since I'm new. Can you think of someone who has standing to suggest that he stop, or just close the door?"

2. **Headphones.** Headphones are God's gift to us for dealing with socially inappropriate coworkers, and you should take advantage of this gift if you can.

34. You've been missing lots of work and know you need to explain it

If you've been missing a lot of work—because of sickness or appointments or something in your personal life—you might be tempted to just stay quiet about it and hope your boss doesn't notice. But you're generally better off raising it yourself so that you can give your boss context for the absences. If you don't do that, she may draw her own conclusions, and they won't necessarily be the right ones. (For example, she could mistakenly think that you're becoming disengaged from work, interviewing for other jobs, or simply being irresponsible about your projects.)

Say something like this:

- *"I know I've missed a lot of work recently. I've been dealing with a health situation that's been requiring a lot of doctors' appointments and sick days, but I'm hopeful that I'll have it under control soon. I wanted to let you know what's going on so that you don't wonder."*

Note that you don't need to get into many specifics here—something like "a health situation" is sufficient. You just want to let her know that there's a reasonable explanation for what's happening and you're not playing hooky.

35. Your boss makes you feel guilty for using your vacation time

Your vacation time is part of your compensation package, and you shouldn't feel guilty about using it. Despite that, though, some managers act as if wanting some time off is the act of a slacker and discourage people from ever getting away from work.

If you have a manager who frowns every time you mention time off or who always seems to have a reason why now isn't the right time to get vacation approved, address it head-on! Here's what to say:

- *"I couldn't tell if you were joking or not when you called me a slacker for asking for vacation time. I assume it's fine for us to use the vacation time the company gives us in our benefits package, but was there something you wanted me doing differently?"*

- *"I haven't been able to have a vacation in almost two years because it's been so hard to find a time when I could go. That's not sustainable in the long term and it's important to me to have time away to recharge. I also want to be able to use the benefits the company is providing as part of our compensation. Can we talk about how to arrange things so that I can get some real time off in the next few months?"*

- *"I hear you that July won't be an ideal time for me to be gone. But it wasn't a good time the last couple of times I've requested vacation, either. I think there's probably never going to be a great time for me to be away, but it's important to me to have real time off. Can we figure out what the least bad option will be, and then I'll make sure that I leave things as covered as possible in my absence? Otherwise I think I'll never be able to take time off, and that's not realistic."*

36. You cried in front of your boss

I have had a *lot* of people cry in my office at work. It's not because I'm a terrifying person who makes people cry; it's because a lot more people cry at work than you probably realize. In fact, in my experience, the more seriously people take their jobs, the more likely they are to cry at work at some point. After all, if you care about your job, the stakes feel high, and when things aren't going the way you want, you can feel frustrated, upset, or disappointed—all of which are known to produce tears. Work isn't some magically emotion-free zone where that never happens.

That said, it's still pretty embarrassing to cry in front of your boss. If it happens, you have a few options.

If the tears are pretty minor, you can say something like:

- *"I'm sorry, I'm feeling really stressed about this. Please ignore this reaction."*

If you'd do better with some time to compose yourself, it's okay to say:

- *"I'm sorry, this is hitting me hard for some reason. Would you mind if I step out for a minute to get a drink of water?"*

If you didn't say anything in the moment, you can always address it the next day or whenever you talk again, by saying something like:

- *"I'm a bit embarrassed that I had such a strong reaction yesterday, and I hope you'll excuse it. I want you to know that I really appreciate the conversation and I'm thinking through what we talked about."* (The idea here is that you don't want your boss to worry that you were so emotional that you didn't fully process whatever the conversation was about.)

A special note if the crying happened while your boss was giving you some difficult feedback about your work: In this case, the danger is that your manager might think that you have trouble hearing critical feedback, which can make her more hesitant to give you feedback in the future or cause her to worry that you're too thin-skinned for discussions of where you could be doing better. That makes it important that you demonstrate that those ideas aren't true and that you are indeed hearing and acting on the feedback. For example, you might send her an email saying something like:

- *"I really appreciate the suggestions you shared with me yesterday, and I'm thinking about how I can better implement them in my work."*

37. Your employer is breaking the law

If your workplace is doing something that violates the law—such as not paying you on time or treating you differently because of your religion—you have the option to go straight to a lawyer or file a complaint with the relevant state or federal agency. However, you can often resolve the situation and still stay on good terms with your employer just by having a straightforward conversation, whereas jumping straight to legal action—while certainly your prerogative—can make your work environment so adversarial that it becomes tricky for you to stay there.

The key is to start from the assumption that your employer doesn't *realize* that they're breaking the law and that you are kindly making them aware of a problem that they will of course want to fix. This is a good approach even if you're pretty sure that your employer is well aware of what they're doing, because framing your language this way will usually get you a better outcome than if you signal that you think they're unrepentant scofflaws.

For example:

- *"We're actually required by federal law to pay overtime to people in my job. I can work the extra hours if you'd like me to, but I want to make sure we don't get in trouble for not paying overtime the way we're required to."*

- *"Rosh Hashanah is a religious holiday for me and I need to attend synagogue services. I know you've asked me to work that day, but federal law says that we're required to accommodate employees' religious practices, and I don't want us to get in trouble."*

- *"We could get into trouble if we don't report my wages. We're required by law to take payroll taxes out of my checks."*

- *"Legally we can't hand out assignments by gender. We'd get into a lot of trouble under federal law if we did that!"*

The important thing to note here is the tone: It's collaborative, not adversarial. A big part of the reason for that is the use of "we" rather than "you" in talking about the company's legal obligations. The idea is that your tone and your framing should convey that you're looking out for the company's interests, not making an overt legal threat.

To be clear, you have every right to make an overt legal threat if you want to. But by starting out this way, you significantly raise your chances of getting the outcome you want while still preserving a good relationship with your employer. If this conversation doesn't work, then you can always escalate to legal action—but starting like this gives you a good chance that you won't.

38. You can't afford the pricey team lunches your office has every month

Presumably you go to work to earn money, not to spend it, so it can be particularly frustrating when meeting basic work expectations comes with a price tag. In some cases, this culture is driven by the employees themselves—for example, if you're surrounded by people who love having regular team lunches where everyone pays her own way without thinking about whether everyone really wants that financial obligation. In other cases, it's driven by managers who are oblivious to the financial realities of more junior staff.

If your office regularly expects you to attend events that cost money that you'd prefer not to shell out, speaking up can feel really awkward, especially if everyone else seems to enjoy the activity. A lot of us feel weird about discussing money, especially when it's to say "I can't afford this thing that you apparently think should be no big deal for me to pay for."

But an even halfway decent boss would want to know if this type of thing is causing hardship. Decent bosses don't want people to blow their budgets to attend a working lunch—and, after you nudge them, will also realize that you might not be the only one who's uncomfortable with the price tag. So when you approach your boss, don't think of it as being a disclosure about your personal finances. Think of it as helping him realize that a work event isn't working the way it was intended to. Here's what you can say:

- *"I really enjoy our team meetings, but the cost of a monthly lunch out isn't in my budget. Is there some way we could do our meetings without cost to employees?"*

Or, if you'd be glad to continue the lunches if they were held at a more affordable restaurant, sometimes suggesting other options can solve the problem:

- *"Would you be open to doing our team lunches at a different restaurant? The price point of the places we've been going is high for me. But I know that Thai Express has a really affordable lunch buffet, and the sandwich place across the street has a great menu and huge tables we could use."*

39. You want to get out of an after-hours social event

Lots of offices assume that everyone will be enthusiastic about the prospect of hanging out with coworkers after hours—whether it's happy hour, a team dinner, trivia night, or what have you. These events are generally intended to boost team morale and cohesion, but plenty of people aren't all that enthused about adding another obligation to their calendar or spending additional time with colleagues they see every day. Fellow introverts, people with childcare obligations or long commutes, and those of you who would just prefer to go home and collapse on the couch, you all have my sympathy in the face of the "obligatory fun" demands that your office might make of you.

But generally, you *can* get out of most after-hours office social events.

The easiest way to do it is to say that you have another commitment. This one is the easiest to pull off, because it's hardest to argue with. You can simply say:

- *"I have an appointment after work that day that I can't move."* (And hey, maybe your appointment is an appointment with yourself on the couch; they don't need to know that.)

- *"I have a family commitment that I can't get out of."*

Or you can say that this particular event isn't your thing:

- *"Happy hours aren't my thing, but I'll see everyone tomorrow."*

- *"Bowling isn't really my bag, but I'm excited to hang out with you all at the retreat next month."*

Or you can joke about it:

- *"I'm going to give you all a break from my devastating charm tonight, but I'll be back in full force tomorrow."*

Or consider just being honest. If your office has a lot of after-hours social events and you get the sense that your manager is wondering why you're never there, it might make sense to say something like this:

- *"I know our team does a lot of stuff together after hours. It's hard for me to attend those because of X, and I wanted to be up-front with you about that so you're not worrying that it reflects my unhappiness with my job or our team."*

Of course, if X is "childcare responsibilities" or "a class I'm taking at night" or something else straightforward, it'll be pretty easy to fill in. But if X is "I'm exhausted at the end of the day and don't really want to hang out with coworkers," you could say it this way:

- *"It's hard for me to attend those because I tend to need to recharge at the end of the day"* . . . or, if you prefer, the vaguer *"I tend to have a lot of stuff scheduled in the evenings."*

I'm being penalized for not participating in monthly athletic events at work

A reader writes:

I work on a team of fifteen people in a large office. My manager came to our team about a year ago. She is young and very athletic, into running marathons, snow-boarding, hiking, etc. She is also very into team-building activities, and that's where my problem comes in. She states she cannot make them mandatory, but one other coworker and I are the only ones who do not participate. I am not against these activities; I used to enjoy them. But with her, every activity has to be extreme and sporty. There was the ten-mile hike, the 5K run, the rock climbing, the parasailing . . . I'm sure you get the idea.

I have some health problems and cannot do activities like these. I suggested low-impact activities like a board game day or a BBQ in the park, and she shot me down without even putting it to a vote with the rest of the team, saying those ideas are not exciting enough.

Each month that we have one of these activities and I do not show up, she writes on my monthly review that I was not a team player and refused to participate in team-building activities. I have privately conferred with the one other employee who also doesn't participate, and the same is done to him. She is a good manager otherwise, but I am quite angry that points are being deducted from my performance review because my body can't hack a 10K hike or run.

Should I speak to her directly and ask her to leave these out of my reviews? Should I take this to HR? I am hesitant to be the office tattletale, but I know upper management does not know these things go on and I am sure that at least half of the activities she's hosted would be prohibited if HR knew.

Ugh, this is such crap. There's no reason that you should be getting penalized on a performance review for not participating in athletic activities, assuming that you are not in fact a professional marathon runner or rock climber.

Have you told her directly that you would like to participate but cannot because of health restrictions? If you haven't, it's time to be more clear with her. As in: "I would really like to participate in team-building activities [*this is you being a good team player*], but I have health restrictions that mean I can't take part in things like running and rock climbing [*this is you presenting highly sound reasoning*]. I'd like to be able to fully participate [*look, it's you emphasizing you're a team player again*], so would it be possible to plan activities that aren't based on sports?"

It's hard to argue that you're not a team player when you're directly asking for activities that you can participate in.

And you also need to say something like: "I don't think that my health restrictions should be a factor in my performance reviews. Can those be revisited?"

The mention of health issues should snap her into consciousness. She should already realize that she's way over the line for penalizing someone for not participating in physical activities unrelated to the core of his job, but the health factor should make her realize that she's also messing with legal issues. If she's not responsive to that, at that point you do need to talk to someone in HR, because what your manager is doing isn't okay and it's worth having someone in a position of authority intervene and point that out to her.

(To be clear, if you weren't being penalized in your performance assessments for not participating, I wouldn't advocate going to HR; I'd just advocate being disgusted with her judgment. But you're being penalized in a way that matters, and that makes it serious business.)

For the record, you shouldn't need to cite health issues to opt out of this never-ending barrage of athleticism. No sane person could argue with health and safety, so you might as well raise it—but as a separate issue, this constant bombardment of mandatory nonwork activities in the guise of team building is a sign of poor judgment, and it raises the question of why she's relying so heavily on it. What's fun for some people is often miserable for others, and mandatory bonding alienates many people, which is the opposite of what it's supposed to do. And that's especially true when the activities are physically grueling ones, which not everyone can or does enjoy.

Add in penalizing people who don't participate, and you have a real clusterfudge of bad judgment.

40. You're going through a hard time in your personal life

If you're going through a rough time personally—a breakup, a family health crisis, or whatever it might be—sometimes it can be useful to tip your boss off, so that she has context if she notices it impacting your work or your demeanor. For example:

- *"I want to let you know that I'm dealing with some diffi-cult things in my personal life right now. I'm doing my best to keep it from affecting my work, but I wanted you to know what's going on in case you notice I seem a little off."*

That's the vague version. If you're comfortable with it, it's fine to be more specific. You don't want to give your boss all the details of your divorce, of course, but it's okay to specify that the personal crisis is a divorce (or that your parent is ill, or you've had your own alarming health news, or whatever the situation may be).

And really, most managers will be concerned for you, will appreciate knowing what's going on, and will want to try to find ways to make your life a little easier if they can.

41. You want time off for therapy

I hear from a lot of people who feel uncomfortable asking their managers about time off to attend therapy. The reason this feels especially tricky is because it's generally a weekly or biweekly appointment and so you can't just ask for an hour or two here and there; you typically need a standing arrange-ment.

The good news is that you absolutely, 100 percent do not need to confide in your boss about your therapy. You can simply say this:

- *"I have a weekly medical appointment for the foreseeable future. It needs to be during weekday hours, but I'll be glad to make up the time each week, of course. Do you have any preference about what day I schedule it for and whether I do it in the morning or the afternoon?"*

You can apply this language to other types of standing medical appointments, too. You don't need to give your boss details, and a savvy boss won't ask for them.

42. You want to recommend a friend for an opening on your team

First, a note of caution: Don't recommend a friend for a job at your company just because she's a friend. Your own professional reputation is going to be on the line when you vouch for someone, so you want to make sure that you genuinely do think that the friend would be a good fit. You don't want to end up being the person who recommended the new hire who sleeps at her desk all day or shouts at the boss.

But if you can attest that your friend is qualified, smart, and easy to work with, and you're willing to stake a bit of your own reputation on the recommendation, then most managers will be glad to get a personal referral from an employee who's in good standing.

Just make sure that you're clear about the limitations of your knowledge. For example, if you've never worked with your friend before, be sure to make that clear. In that case, you could say something like:

- *"My friend Valentina Warbleworth applied for the community outreach job. I've never worked with her, so I can't vouch for her outreach qualifications, but I can tell you that she's smart, funny, a terrific writer, and she's great at connecting with people."* (Fill in whatever things about your friend make you think she'd be a good fit.)

And in cases where you *have* worked with the friend, make sure you specify that, too, since it will give the recommendation additional weight. In that case, you could say something like:

- *"My friend Valentina Warbleworth applied for the community outreach job, and I think she could be a really strong candidate. We used to work together on the clean water campaign, and she was one of the stars of the office—a great writer and fantastic at building coalitions. She would definitely be worth talking to."*

43. Your boss is considering hiring someone you used to work with and can't stand

Most managers are very interested in hearing input from current employees who know a candidate they're considering hiring, especially if you worked with the person in the past. Hiring is far from a perfect science, and so getting candid input from people who know candidates firsthand can be hugely valuable. As long as you're in reasonably good standing with your boss, your opinion is likely to carry a fair amount of weight.

The key here is to get as specific as you can about why the person would be a bad hire. "I don't really like him" isn't helpful. "He didn't pull his weight on group projects and was rude to interns" or "He was prickly to the point of being hard to approach for assistance" is significantly more useful.

Ideally, if your manager knows that you worked together in the past, she'll solicit your input. But if she doesn't, raise it yourself by saying something like:

- *"Tad and I actually worked together in the past, and I'd have some concerns about his fit for this job. Can I tell you a little about my experience working with him?"*

44. Your boss is misrepresenting a job on your team to candidates in interviews

When you're interviewing for a job, you damn well hope people are straightforward with you about what you'd be signing on for so that you don't end up in a position that makes you miserable. So it can be deeply unsettling if you're helping your boss interview candidates for a job on your team and realize that he's misleading candidates about the position, the department culture, or his own management style.

The easiest one of these to tackle is if you disagree with the way he's describing the job itself, since that's likely to feel less personal to him than the culture or his own style. You can try approaching that just as a straightforward difference in perspective about what the work entails. For example:

- *"I noticed you described the work as being primarily writing and editing, with very little admin support work. I think there's actually a sizable component of admin work to the job. I know when Portia was doing it, she spent probably twenty percent of her time on scheduling, answering the phone, and other admin stuff. Would it make sense to adjust how we're describing the position to candidates?"* (Notice the very handy "we" there, which puts you both on the same side.)

If the issue is the way your boss is describing the culture, now we're heading into territory that might feel a bit more personal. In that case, you might frame it this way:

- *"You know, I don't know that I'd describe our culture as super-flexible. I certainly don't think it's unacceptably rigid or anything like that, but I think when people hear 'flexible,' they're picturing things like flexible hours and the ability to work from home. That's not really us, and I worry about giving people the wrong impression and then having them be disappointed once they're on the job and realize we don't do those things."*

But what if the issue is how your boss is describing himself? For example, what if he's telling candidates that he gives people lots of autonomy when you know that in reality he's prone to micromanaging? You probably don't want to say, "Actually, you're a terrible micromanager." But you could say something like this:

- *"For what it's worth, I don't know if I'd describe your style as being one that gives people a ton of autonomy. I think you like to be pretty hands-on, which is fine and I can see why it often makes sense with the type of work that we do. But I worry that if we set candidates up to expect a high degree of autonomy, we might inadvertently end up hiring someone to whom that's really important and who might be frustrated by the way we work."*

Be sure to say this in a nonjudgmental tone so that it doesn't sound like criticism (throwing in "It's fine and makes sense for our work" can help greatly with that, even if it's a bit of a white lie for our purposes here) and to frame it in terms of "Let's hire someone who's right for how we work." (Notice there's the handy "we" again. "We" is possibly the most helpful word you'll ever use when talking to your boss.)

45. You want to work from home

In some offices, getting permission to work remotely is as simple as asking and explaining your reasoning. For example:

- *"I find that it's tough to concentrate on work that requires deep focus when I'm in the office. Would it be okay if I worked from home a few times a month when I have something that requires more uninterrupted concentration? It would have been really helpful to be able to do that last month when I was writing the pitch to the watermelon growers' association, for instance."* (Note that you're specifying frequency here. That's because you want to make sure that you're both envisioning the same thing in that regard, and that she doesn't think she's okaying telecommuting once a month while you're picturing doing it twice a week.)

But if your boss is resistant to telecommuting on principle—if she's one of those managers who's skeptical about whether people work as hard when they're at home, or worries that it will inhibit collaboration or inconvenience her or others—then you'll need to do more convincing. As we talked about at the beginning of this chapter, this is a case where you might have better luck asking for a limited-time experiment than a permanent change.

In that case, you could say:

- *"I know you're not convinced that working from home makes sense for our team. Would you be open to trying a short-term experiment and then revisiting it once we have real-life data to work with? If you're willing to test it, I could try working from home a couple of times this month, and then we could talk about how it went. My hope is that there's a way to do it smoothly without any negative impact on anyone, but I know that I can't say for sure until we try it. If we do try it and it causes problems, we could of course put it to rest at that point. But if it works, I think it could really benefit everyone, and even be something that helps attract and retain good people in the future since it's something that so many people want these days and that more and more companies are offering."*

46. Your boss won't honor something you negotiated

When you negotiate special terms with an employer as part of accepting a job offer—like an extra week of vacation or the ability to work from home one day a week—you generally assume that the employer will honor that agreement. But sometimes things change—a new manager comes in and doesn't want to honor your initial agreement, or the company decides to ban remote workdays officewide. If you have your agreement in writing, that might give you some protection, but if that doesn't protect you (or you never got it in writing), what should you do?

If your boss is at least semi-sane, try saying something like this:

- *"I asked for _____ to be included in my job offer because it's important to me. I understand that circumstances may have changed, but this was a key part of why I accepted the offer originally, so withdrawing it would represent a significant change in my compensation. Can we talk about ways we might be able to continue to make our initial agreement work?"*

The key elements to stress here are that you relied on your employer's promise when accepting the offer and that it was a significant factor in your decision.

Ultimately, if your manager won't budge, you may need to decide whether you want the job on these new terms. But try pushing back first and see where that gets you.

I had to share a bed with a coworker on a business trip

A reader writes:
Some coworkers and I recently went on overnight travel, and the plan was to have us split two hotel rooms. Sharing a room with people I work with is not my favorite thing, but we're a nonprofit and we do this to save money, so I grit my teeth and vent later, if needed, to friends and family.

I expected this trip would follow the standard room sharing format, and that I would probably end up sharing a room with my boss. However, there were some unexpected changes that ultimately resulted in three people sharing one room with two beds. Those last two points I did not realize until the moment we walked into the room. My stomach dropped when I saw the beds.

I hope it doesn't require much explanation to convey how very, very upset I was to have to share what amounted to every last inch of personal space. It's bad enough to lose any potential downtime during these trips because I am sharing a room with a coworker who snores or talks in her sleep or gets up an hour before I need to, or who simply by virtue of her presence means I won't be able to take my brain out of work mode after a twelve- or fourteen-hour day. But to share a bed?! There is a very, very short list of people I want to share a bed with, and no matter how much I will ever like the people I work with, they will never, ever be on that list.

I plan to bring this up with my boss, but I'm having difficulty finding words that would be effective when I'm the only person who seems to find what happened unreasonable and unprofessional. Do you have any advice you could share on how to bring this up like a calm and reasonable adult?

Your letter has given me nightmares.

Under no circumstances is it reasonable to expect you to share a bed with a coworker.

Good lord.

Was the front desk not willing to send up a cot, at least?

In any case, yes, yes, yes, speak to your boss. Say this: "Somehow on our last trip, three of us were booked into a room with only two beds, and Jane and I had to sleep in the same bed. I don't know if it was intentionally booked that way or if it was a fluke. I'm not comfortable sharing a bed with a coworker, and I'm sure others aren't either. I want to make sure we're not intentionally booking people that way. Also, if it somehow happens again, I want to make sure it's okay for me to expense a separate room at the hotel for one of the people."

I don't think she'll push back too strongly, because sharing a bed with colleagues is not normal, but if she does, say this: "I'm just not comfortable with it and don't want to do it again." If necessary, you can add, "Sleeping in the same bed with someone is an intimate activity, and we can't require employees to do that."

This is a reasonable position to draw a line on.

As for the room sharing, separate from the bed sharing ... It is true that there are some industries where sharing hotel *rooms* is the norm, including academia and some nonprofits, but frankly I think there are times when it's reasonable to push back on that as well. I come from nonprofits too, and I get the desire to be responsible with money—and I shared some hotel rooms with coworkers in my twenties, so I know that it's a thing that happens, although Never Again, Holy Hell, No, Never Again—but there's a point where it's just not reasonable to ask that of people, especially senior people, and especially on particularly draining trips or when there would be three of you (!) in the room. You know your organization best, so you know if there's room to advocate change there, but I wouldn't write it off.

But sharing a bed? Sticking with a flat "I'm not comfortable doing that again" is the way to go here. And then follow through—if you ever find yourself in that situation again, pick up the phone, call the front desk, and get an additional room, or at least a rollaway bed. Part of business travel is that you sometimes need to adjust your travel arrangements on the fly, and discovering that you've been booked into an intimate slumber party certainly qualifies as a good reason.

47. Your boss asks if you're looking for another job

If you're actively job-searching, you might not be ready to tell your boss yet . . . which can make things awkward if he starts asking you about your longer-term plans with the company or even asks you directly whether you're looking for another job.

If you've determined that it's not in your self-interest to disclose your plans to leave your job—for example, if you have reason to think you would be pushed out earlier than you're ready to leave—say something like:

- *"Obviously no one can predict the future, but I don't have any current plans to leave."* (This is true. You don't have any finalized, solid plans to leave.)

- *"Nothing's written in stone, of course, but I'm happy being here."*

- *"If someone came to me with a job that gave me opportunities that I don't have here, I'd have to consider it, but I don't have any current plans to leave."*

48. You're resigning

People *really* agonize over resigning. I get a ton of letters from people who are dreading giving notice at work, and who worry that they'll be inflicting a deeply personal wound on their boss and on their organization.

The good news is, it pretty much never goes down that way. Resigning doesn't need to be a big, difficult conversation at all. In fact, it would be pretty odd if it ended up that way!

All you have to do is ask to talk to your boss in person (or over the phone if you work in different locations) and say this:

- *"I've really enjoyed my time working here. But after a lot of thought, I've made the difficult decision to move on, and my last day will be _____."*

That's it!

Your boss might ask why you're leaving, and you'll want to be prepared with an answer to that, so that you don't end up winging it and accidentally unleashing a tirade about something you didn't mean to bring up. But that answer can be as simple as one of these:

- *"This opportunity fell into my lap and I couldn't pass it up."*

- *"I've learned a lot here, but I felt it was time for me to move on to something new."*

In other words, your answer doesn't have to be a detailed explanation of what really drove you to start looking. Of course, if you want to explain the reason, that's fine too—but know that you don't need to if you'd rather not get into it.

Also, be prepared for the possibility that your boss might ask you if there's anything she can do to get you to stay. In general, it's a bad idea to accept counteroffers, since in most cases the factors that drove you to start looking aren't likely to change. (And even if they are, do you want to have to quit to get the things you want from your employer?) But it's smart to think this possibility through before you resign so that you're not blindsided if it comes up.

What about using a job offer to get a raise or promotion at your current job?

Think carefully before using another job offer as a bargaining chip to get a raise or promotion at your current job. More often than not, you're better off trying to negotiate for a raise or promotion on your own merits (and being willing to move on if you don't get it).

The thing about counteroffers is that employers often make them in a moment of panic about losing someone at a bad time, but in many cases they can fundamentally change the relationship. Once their panic subsides and they've succeeded in keeping you, you're now the person who was looking to leave, and you might be seen as more dispensable if your company needs to make cuts in the future.

And importantly, there are reasons you started job searching in the first place (culture misfit, dislike of your company's management, lack of recognition, and so forth) and those will stay problems after the immediate glow from your raise wears off. Plus, the fact that you needed to have one foot out the door to get paid what you're worth isn't a great sign, and there's no reason to think that future salary increases will be easier. In fact, the next time you ask for a raise, you might hear, "We just gave you that big raise when you were thinking about leaving."

And of course, if you use a job offer to try to get your company to counter, there's no guarantee that you won't hear, "We can't match that, so go ahead and take it."

(Caveat: There *are* some industries where using counteroffers is an accepted method of getting a raise or promotion, but make very sure that you're in one before proceeding that way!)

49. Your manager responds badly to your resignation

Most managers react to resignations with disappointment but acceptance. It's never great news to hear that a valued employee is leaving, but it's also a normal part of doing business, and most managers—even if disappointed—won't berate you or yell at you.

But that's "most," not all. Some managers do take resignations personally and react inappropriately. (I once had a manager lock me in her office for two hours while she lectured me about how I was betraying the organization by leaving. This was pretty early in my career, or I would have known that I could get up and leave!) If you encounter a manager who reacts badly, remember that your decision to leave and the timing of your departure are entirely up to you. Your boss can't make you stay, or delay your departure, if you don't want to. You're not an indentured servant!

If your manager gives you a hard time about your resignation, stay cheerful, upbeat, and firm, and say something like this:

- *"I appreciate that you want to keep me. But I've given it a lot of thought and this is the right decision for me. June 15 will be my last day. Let's talk about what I can do between now and then to make the transition as smooth as possible."*

If your boss keeps pushing after that, repeat this as necessary:

- *"I've thought it over and my decision is final."*

If things become really uncomfortable—if, say, your boss is openly hostile—you can always say something like this:

- *"I'd like to work out my final two weeks and leave things in good shape, but I'm not comfortable with the way you're talking to me. Do you think we can work together civilly for this period, or should we move up my ending date?"*

You could even change that last part to:

- *"We either need to work together civilly or today will need to be my last day."*

But you might be able to preserve the relationship, and the reference, by using the slightly softer first approach.

50. You think you're in danger of being fired

Worrying that you might be fired is a terrible feeling. If you seriously believe that you're in danger of being fired (as opposed to just having an anxiety freak-out that isn't rooted in real evidence), one option is to talk to your boss and put your worries on the table. Say something like this:

- *"I wonder if we could talk about how things are going. I know I've had some struggles and haven't picked up on the job as quickly as I think you were expecting me to. I'm working really hard on the things you've asked me to do differently, and I'm hopeful that I'm going to be able to hit the bar you need. But I know that your concerns are serious ones, and I don't want to bury my head in the sand. Is your sense that I'm likely to be able to get to where you need me to be?"*

Depending on what the issues are, it's possible that you'll hear something that will reassure you—like that everyone struggles when learning this role, or that you've shown enough improvement that your boss is confident that things will work out.

But it's also possible that you'll hear a pretty bleak assessment of your chances. If that happens, one option is to respond with something like this:

- *"I really appreciate your being candid with me. Given that assessment, I wonder if we could plan for a transition that gives me some time to look for another job and gives you some time to search for a replacement as well. Maybe that could be the best outcome for both of us."*

A lot of managers are likely to be relieved at this kind of proposal. Few managers want to fire someone if it can be avoided, so if you make it easy for your boss to end the relationship without firing you, you can often get some things that help you: time to look for a new job while you're still employed, not having a firing on your record, and having more control over the situation than you otherwise might.

However, there's a big caveat here: There's a risk that this conversation could prompt your manager to fire you more quickly than he otherwise would have, now that the subject has been raised. So you need to balance that possibility against the benefits of being able to talk about the situation openly.

CHAPTER 2

Conversations with Your Coworkers

Relationships with coworkers can be tricky. You spend an enormous amount of time around them, but you generally don't get to choose who they are. There's professional pressure to maintain reasonably good relations with them, which means that you can't always speak your mind in the way that you might with friends or family—and yet their behavior can have a huge impact on your quality of life at work, and sometimes on your work itself. On top of that, there are often internal politics to navigate, which can make even the most straightforward conversations feel fraught.

Given all of this, it's understandable that you might be hesitant to raise an issue with a coworker. But so often, just approaching the problem in the right way will get you the results you want without introducing the kind of tension you might fear. In this chapter, I'm going to give you specific wording to help you do that.

First, though, I want to lay out some key principles that you can use whenever you need to approach a coworker about something uncomfortable:

- **Use the same tone you would use to raise any other work-related problem.** You want to use the same tone that you'd use to say, "Hey, I'm having trouble opening the spreadsheets you're sending me—can you help me figure out why?" Using that kind of tone—as opposed to a hesitant "I feel super-awkward about saying this" tone—makes your coworker more likely to respond in kind.

- **Put yourself in the other person's shoes.** If you were doing something that really annoyed a coworker, wouldn't you want to know? Even if the conversation is a little awkward in the moment, some passing awkwardness is probably preferable to staying oblivious to something that's driving someone batty, especially if you can easily change your behavior.

- **In most cases, you should try to talk to your coworker directly before escalating the situation to your manager.** There *are* times when you should loop in your manager: if the problem is a very serious one (such as reporting sexual harassment or a coworker who's cheating a client) or one that recurs after you attempt to address it on your own. But if the issue is more of an interpersonal one, your manager is likely to want you to address it on your own, at least to start. And really, you'd probably want someone to talk to you directly before escalating a concern to your boss, so it's good to give your coworker that same consideration (again, with exceptions for very serious situations).

- **Own the message.** Sometimes people are tempted to borrow the authority of a group when delivering a difficult message, which leads them to say things like "You're annoying everyone when you get so off-topic at meetings" or "None of us like having potlucks this often." But even if you know that others feel the same as you, framing things as if you're speaking for a group can alienate the person you're talking to. (You wouldn't be thrilled to hear that a group of people had been complaining to each other about you, after all.) This framing also can derail the message you're delivering if the person knows there's at least one other person who doesn't agree with you. It's okay to just speak on behalf of yourself ("I'd rather not have potlucks so frequently").

- **Sometimes being self-deprecating can make things easier.** If you're worried that the message you want to deliver will come across as "There's something wrong with you," sometimes you can effectively reframe it as "This is just a weird thing about me." For example, if you want to ask a touchy-feely coworker to stop hugging you all the time, you *could* say, "Please stop hugging me"—but it'll probably cast a chill on the relationship. You'll likely cause less awkwardness if you instead say something like, "Hey, I'm not a hugger. I know you mean it warmly; I'm just not very touchy-feely." Framing it as "It's me, not you" gets you results with minimal awkwardness. And if it doesn't work, you can always take a more serious approach.

Important caveat here: This tactic makes sense in some situations and not in others. You needn't pretend it's your own idiosyncrasy that makes you not want to, say, hear racist comments.

- **Try to make things normal afterward.** After an awkward or difficult conversation, try to find an opportunity soon afterward to have a normal conversation with the person about something else. That will reinforce that you're not upset and hopefully will help to reset the dynamic.

- **Not *every* issue needs to be raised.** Working with other humans means that you're going to be around other people's annoying habits. It's okay to speak up when something makes it harder for you to do your job, seriously impacts your quality of life, or has unintended consequences. But some annoying things that coworkers do come with the territory of working in an office. If the offending behavior is relatively minor, sometimes it just makes sense to live with it, or at least to try for a while before deciding you can't.

1. Your coworker is doing something loud and annoying

One of the more frequent complaints that I receive at Ask a Manager is "My coworker is doing something loud and annoying"—from playing music without headphones to taking too many calls on speakerphone to humming incessantly. These things might sound relatively small, but when you're trapped in close proximity to them, they can become truly aggravating over time. And there's no end to the annoying noises other people can make when we're trying to concentrate. (I once received a letter from someone who wrote of her gum-chewing coworker, "I can hear the gum sloshing in her mouth and the tiny pops that she makes with it.")

Most people don't realize they are making noise and will be receptive to a polite request to stop. You can say it this way:

- *"I'm finding it hard to focus when I can hear your music. Could you try using headphones?"* (If you want to soften this, try: *"I actually really like your music, but it makes it hard for me to concentrate."* It's hard to get defensive when someone is complimenting you.)

- *"You probably don't realize this, but you have a habit of drumming your fingers on your desk for much of the day. I've tried to block it out, but it's pretty distracting. Would you mind putting down something soft to reduce the noise it makes?"*

- *"I know it's weird, but the sound of gum popping is like nails on a blackboard to me. Any chance you can try not to pop it?"*

If you're worried that you'll sound too nitpicky, a good tactic can be to poke fun at yourself a bit while you're asking— e.g., "I'm bizarrely sensitive to sound" or "I have a weird hang-up about gum noises." By signaling that you haven't lost perspective, you're decreasing the likelihood that the other person will get defensive (since now it's about you, not him).

2. Your coworker isn't pulling her weight on projects you're both responsible for

There's a reason so many people hate group work in school— one person often gets stuck with most of the work. Unfortunately, it's not always different in the work world; sometimes your success depends on someone else, and that someone else isn't coming through.

If your coworker is slacking off on projects you're both responsible for, you may need to talk to your boss about what's going on. But before you do that, try talking to your coworker directly. When you do, focus on the impact of what's been happening. It's not about your coworker being lazy; it's about how it's impacting your part of the work.

- If you've already covered your coworker's part of the work: *"Hey, my understanding was that I'd cover X and you'd cover Y but I ended up doing both last week since we were so close to the deadline and Y wasn't done. Can you tell me what happened?"*

- If your coworker's part is still not done: *"We can't move forward with X until you handle Y. Do you know when it'll be done?"*

- If it's been happening over and over: *"I keep not being able to move forward with my parts of the project because I'm waiting on pieces from you. I know that you have other things going on, but I'm worried about the impact the delays are having. Is there something we can do differently so that we're reliably hitting the deadlines we've set for ourselves?"*

- And if you're ready to get even more serious about it: *"I know you're busy, but when you don't cover your pieces of the project, I end up doing them myself or we get into a schedule crunch. It's happened enough times that I think we need to change something about how we're tackling the work. If you don't have the time to do your pieces, could we talk to Jane about making other arrangements for them?"*

3. Your coworker constantly complains about her job or your boss

Everybody vents about work now and then. But when you work with someone who's constantly unleashing a stream of negativity about her job, your company, and/or your boss, it can get really old really quickly. It's exhausting to be around that kind of negativity, and it can make small problems start to feel like bigger ones.

If you've listened to a coworker vent in the past, it can feel tough to ask her to stop now. But honestly, it's okay to do that! You can frame it in terms of your own quality of life at work:

- *"I know you're pretty frustrated about things here. I honestly don't have the same concerns, but it's starting to pull me into a place of negativity too. Can we try to rein in the negative talk about work and talk about other things instead? I'd really appreciate it."*

- *"I'm finding that talking about work frustrations so frequently is starting to impact how I feel about coming to work every day, and I don't want that! I'm trying to be more positive and focus on the things I like here instead."*

A totally different approach is to ask your coworker this the next time he complains:

- *"So what do you plan to do about it?"*

You can then follow that up with:

- *"You sound pretty unhappy and have been venting to me for a while. Are you at the point where you're considering what you're going to do about it?"*

If you consistently move the conversation in that direction, your coworker will figure out pretty quickly that you're not a satisfying person to vent to anymore . . . or who knows, he may actually take the advice and start thinking about what to do about the situation!

4. Your coworker won't stop talking to you while you're trying to concentrate

Getting an overly chatty coworker to cut back on the chit-chat tends to require multiple conversations: first explaining that you aren't available to talk as much as she'd like, and then ongoing reinforcement until the message sticks.

Step 1: Cut the coworker off in the moment. For example:

- *"I'm actually just in the middle of finishing something, so I should get back to it."*

Or try a white lie, like:

- *"I've got to get ready for a phone call that's about to come in"* or *"Can't talk—I'm on deadline."*

Step 2: If addressing individual instances as they occur doesn't get the message across, your next step is to address the larger pattern:

- *"I like talking with you, but it's hard for me to do much of that during the workday. I usually need to get back to work pretty quickly."* If you do genuinely enjoy your co-worker's company, you could add: *"I'd love to get coffee with you sometime, but I've got to do a better job of not letting us get into longer conversations when I should be working."*

- *"I'm finding that the amount we talk during the day is preventing me from getting my work done, so I need to really cut down on how much chitchat we have."*

- *"I know we're both in the habit of chatting a lot, so going forward, I'm going to be really vigilant about not doing that. I'm mentioning it now, because I don't want you to think I'm being chilly when I can't talk as frequently."*

- When the problem is less about lengthy social conversations and more about multiple small interruptions: *"I'm finding I need long uninterrupted stretches in order to stay focused. I want to make sure you get your questions answered, though, so what if we schedule one or two meetings a week to talk and save things up for those?"*

Step 3: Now you've put her on notice that you need to chat less. So when she starts chatting with you again, be direct and be firm:

- *"Sorry, gotta stay focused here."*

- *"Working over here!"*

- *"Dude, you are going to destroy my ability to finish this press release. I'm shutting you out!"*

- *"I'm on deadline—let's talk later."*

5. Your coworker's constant personal calls are making it hard to focus on your work

If your coworker's personal conversations are interfering with your ability to get work done, you have to speak up. Start with this:

- *"I know you have to take a lot of personal calls during the day. I'm finding that's making it really hard for me to focus on my work. I don't know if there's a way for you to take the calls somewhere else, or if there's something else we might try? I'm sorry to ask this and I want to be sensitive to your needs, too, but I'm really having trouble concentrating some days."*

If it continues after that, it's time to be very specific about what you'd like your coworker to do differently:

- *"Sorry to raise this again, but your calls are still really distracting. Could you please take them away from your desk if there's going to be more than one or two a day?"*

If that doesn't work, then the next step is to talk with your manager. If you feel weird about doing that, keep in mind that this isn't just an interpersonal issue; it's something that's impacting your ability to do your job. You can be pretty blunt:

- *"Kyle is on pretty frequent personal calls throughout the day, and it's making it tough to concentrate. I've tried using headphones and I've tried asking him to take the calls away from our work area, but it hasn't solved the problem. Is there somewhere else I could sit, or is it possible for you to ask him to take those calls away from his desk?"*

6. You need shorter answers from a long-winded coworker

Trying to get a quick answer out of someone who's long-winded and prone to rambling is one of work life's constant frustrations (at least for me; I'm an impatient person). But if you're willing to be direct about what you need from the person, there's actually some hope of keeping your exchanges to a more reasonable length.

The first thing you can do when you know that you're dealing with a rambler is to try to head it off at the very start of the conversation by saying things like:

- *"I only have a minute but wanted to quickly ask you about X."*

- *"I have a lot of questions for you, so I'm going to ask that you focus on top-level responses, and I'll let you know if I need more details."*

- *"Can you give me a brief one-minute overview of X?"*

- *"I know there's a lot to this, so can we start with the quick upshot, and then if I need more details, I'll ask?"*

Then don't be afraid to interrupt and redirect the conversation. This can feel rude because you probably wouldn't normally interrupt a colleague, but if someone is rambling on and on, it's okay to interject to provide more clarity about what will be helpful to you. (And really, most chronic ramblers are pretty used to people jumping in.) For example:

- *"I'm realizing I wasn't clear—I know there's a lot of background here, but what I really need is just X."*

- *"I'm sorry to cut you off, but since I'm in a rush with this one, could we actually just go straight to what the status of X is?"*

- *"Sorry if I wasn't clear—this is actually a lot more than I need! For my purposes, just X would be ideal."*

- *"Actually, since my piece of this is really just X, can we focus on that?"*

7. Coworker keeps giving you last-minute work

When you're given last-minute work that is only last-minute because of someone else's poor planning, it can be tempting to put your foot down and say that you can't accommodate it without more notice. And in some contexts, you can do that. But in other cases, you'd come across as too rigid and out of touch with your employer's priorities if you refused.

But that doesn't mean that you can't say something. If your coworker's delays are both (a) avoidable and (b) hindering your ability to get your other work done, you should speak up.

First, point out the issue, since your coworker who keeps giving you last-minute work may not even realize that what she's doing is a problem:

- *"Is there a way for me to get this type of work earlier? It can take a while to turn it around, and when I have other looming deadlines, it's hard to fit it in when I don't have more notice. Ideally I'd like at least a few days with this kind of thing, since I'm fitting it in around other priorities."*

If it keeps happening after that, address it as it happens:

- *"I can try to fit this in, but I had most of today and tomorrow scheduled for other work. Is there any wiggle room on the deadline for this, since it's coming to me so late?"*

8. Telling a coworker that something isn't your job

There's an old adage that you should never say "That's not my job." And sure, it's true that you shouldn't be rigid about sticking precisely to your job description; most job descriptions evolve and expand over time. But there *are* times when it's appropriate and even necessary to point out that you aren't the right person to do a particular task.

But you shouldn't just say "That's not my job." Instead, you should explain *why* you're not the right person to handle whatever the task is, and when possible, suggest someone who might be.

For example:

- *"I'm on deadline with High Priority X and I've got to stay focused on that so I can't help, unfortunately."*

- *"Ophelia and I decided I needed to focus exclusively on cleaning up the donation backlog this month, so I'm not supposed to be taking on anything else right now."*

- *"Hmm, I'm not usually the person who handles that. I think Pablo is, and he should be able to help you."*

9. Coworker is leaning on you for too much help

You might have been happy to help out your coworker when he was new to the job or just learning a new task, but if he has continued to lean on you for help beyond the point that seems reasonable, it's okay to say something, especially if it's distracting you from your own work.

The easiest option, and the one you should try first, is to stop being so available. Say something like:

- *"I'm sorry, I'm right in the middle of something so I can't help."*

- *"I'm having a hectic day so I can't break from what I'm doing."*

But if that doesn't work, you might need to address it more broadly:

- *"Now that you've got the basics down for how to do this, I need to pull back from helping so much, since my own projects are piling up."*

- *"It's getting tough for me to focus on my work when we're tackling so many questions together, so going forward, can you direct these sorts of questions to [manager]?"*

- *"Can I ask you to start being really vigilant about checking your notes from training before coming to me? If you've reviewed your documentation and are still stuck, I can try to help, but I need to limit it so that I'm able to focus on my own projects. And I think you'll find a lot of the answers in there."*

How do I get my coworkers to stop using me for tech support?

A reader writes:

Do you have any strategies to stop people from using me as the in-house tech support?

I am by far the most technically savvy employee in my firm, and I'm happy to help with complicated or unusual IT requests. Lately, however, people who should have good IT skills are plaguing me with questions about everything from how to make cell borders visible in Excel to how to (no kidding) browse files. Literally, a twenty-something colleague with a degree and recent experience in an office did not know how to browse directories on his computer!

I don't feel I can say I'm on a deadline or can't be interrupted because each request takes only a couple of minutes, but the time adds up and up. I also don't want to pretend to be too busy to stop for a second, because it's an obvious lie if I then take a time-out for a chat.

How do I cut this out? I'm getting increasingly frustrated that I'm doing the same or better work as colleagues on my pay grade, while also showing them basic computer skills they should already know.

Well, first, you absolutely can say that you can't be interrupted even though the request would only take a couple of minutes. It's perfectly fine to say, "Sorry, I've got to finish something up" or "I can't break my focus right now" or "Can't help—having a hectic day."

But I hear you that you want to still be able to chat with people or whatever without looking like you were obviously lying when you declined to help someone out ten minutes ago.

So I'd just tell people that you can't help with this kind of thing anymore and explain why. For instance: "I'm pulling back on helping with this kind of thing because it's started taking up a significant amount of my time. But if you Google the question, you should find lots of help. That's how I've figured out most of this stuff."

Or, if you want to make it clear that you're willing to help on occasion, but only if they've tried to figure out the answer first, you can ask, "What have you tried so far to solve it?" If the answer turns out to be nothing, then you can say, "Do me a favor and Google this stuff before pulling me in—I'm getting a lot of requests for this kind of thing, and I need to limit them. If you've spent more than fifteen minutes trying to figure it out and are still stuck, then feel free to come check with me, but that should solve a lot of them."

But aside from suggesting specific wording, I also want to tell you that a big part of solving this is you *believing* that it's okay to protect your own time and say no to this kind of thing. If you truly internalize that it's okay for you to do that, the sorts of responses above are more likely to come out of your mouth naturally . . . and you'll probably deliver them in the matter-of-fact way that will reinforce to your coworkers that you're not in fact their on-call help desk.

10. Responding to nosy questions

I get an enormous number of questions at Ask a Manager from people wondering how to fend off nosy questions from coworkers—about their love lives, their health, and even their reproductive plans. (I even once received a letter from someone whose coworker said to her, "I noticed you've gone to the restroom a lot today. Everything still working down there?" Shudder.)

If you're faced with overly personal questions at work, the most important thing is to remember that you're not obligated to answer just because they're asking. Often when confronted with inappropriate question askers, people hesitate to shut the conversation down because they don't want to seem rude. But the person demanding answers to intrusive questions is the rude one, not you! It's not discourteous to decline to share personal information.

Some options:

- *"That's awfully personal!"*

- *"Why do you ask?"*

- *"I'd rather not talk about my dating life."*

- *"I'd rather not get into it at work—that topic is pretty personal to me."*

- *"I'm not comfortable talking about that."*

- *"Whoa, getting pretty personal there, huh?"*

These lines will be enough to shut down most nosy people. But if you've got a coworker who still persists, at that point you can say something like:

- *"Please stop asking me that. It's not something I want to discuss at work. Thank you."*

11. You let your frustration get the better of you and were rude to someone

Ideally you'd always maintain your cool when dealing with frustrating coworkers, regardless of the provocation. But because you're human, and because some coworkers are incredibly irritating, it's possible that you might occasionally fall short of this standard.

If it happens, you should apologize. Apologizing doesn't mean that the person wasn't rude or in the wrong herself, but you're still responsible for your own behavior—and in most cases, acknowledging that you snapped and apologizing for that will make you look a lot better (including with any bystanders who might have witnessed it).

There's a pretty straightforward formula you can use if this happens:

- *"I wanted to come by and apologize for snapping at you earlier. I was frustrated with how our conversation was going, but I shouldn't have used that tone with you, and I apologize."*

(Of course, if you find yourself regularly needing to apologize for being rude, that's a red flag that something bigger is going on that you need to resolve.)

My coworker writes
a mean blog about me

A reader writes:

I have a work colleague, "J." J and I sit next to each other and have been friendly the entire time we've worked together. She has told me about things in her personal life and I've shared the same type of stuff with her.

A couple days ago, J showed me something she'd reblogged and I happened to notice the URL of her blog. I looked up her blog later and started reading it; I didn't think I was being out of line since she'd shown me the page already.

Then I found a very recent post where she made fun of me for starting a cleanse. I was hurt, but I was even more hurt to find that her followers were urging her on to create a blog devoted to my "ridiculousness." Apparently she posts about me a lot and the things she writes are very unkind.

Now I'm at a loss as to what to do. I know that the best option is to let this go, back away from the "friendship" gracefully, and not read the blog again. But the extent to which she has posted about me is pretty startling. Worst of all—she's recently posted a conversation we had about our boss, who had to go home for medical reasons. J kept insisting it was because of a prescription drug overdose, and I tried to stop the conversation by saying "I think it's a medical issue" (basically, saying it's private and using my tone to indicate I didn't want to talk about it). But now it's on this blog and it looks like I was participating in gossip.

It's not difficult to find her blog at all, and based on personal information she shares, it's not difficult to identify her or the (small) company that we both work for. Aside from my own anger and hurt over what I've found, the things she posts about could be potentially embarrassing for our employer.

At a minimum, I'd really like her to take the post about our boss down, but I don't know how to broach this topic without blowing things up radically. Do you have any suggestions about how to tackle this diplomatically? Am I being unreasonably sensitive about things she posted in her personal blog (that was probably never meant for me to see)?

J sounds like a jerk.

You're not being unreasonably sensitive. Your co-worker, who you thought you had a warm relationship with, is mocking you to strangers, repeatedly. That's horrible.

I'd say something like this to her: "This is awkward to bring up, but I read some of the blog posts you've written about me and others in the office. I was pretty taken aback. I didn't realize that you felt like that, and I felt pretty awful seeing the things your followers were saying."

Then stop and see what she says. If she has any sense at all, she's going to be mortified. She might tell you that she just does it to blow off steam, or that she doesn't really mean what she posts there. To anything like that, or any kind of defensiveness, I'd just respond, "Well, it was pretty upsetting to see."

Because it *was* upsetting and it's reasonable to tell her that, so that she's face-to-face with the consequences of writing mean things about people online.

There's a good chance that she's going to take all

those posts down now after that conversation (or possibly make the blog private, if that's an option). It would take some serious gall to leave them up. But if she doesn't, or if you don't want to wait to see if she does, you could say, "I'd appreciate it if you'd remove those posts about me" and/or "I really think you should remove the post about [boss]" and/or "For what it's worth, I think the company would be concerned if they ever came across these posts, especially since it's not hard to identify who you work for." But that's really about saving her from herself, and you're not obligated to do that if you don't want to get into that level of discussion with her.

Also: This is going to be an uncomfortable conversation, but it's important to remember that it's her actions that created the discomfort, not yours.

12. Your coworker keeps making judgmental comments about your snacks

I don't know what's up with coworkers who think they're the diet police, but offices across the land are dealing with an epidemic of people who comment on what other people eat. It's not unusual for a candy bar or a bag of chips to draw comments like "Oh, being naughty today?" or "It must be so nice to be able to eat junk like that." And on the other end of the spectrum, if you usually eat healthy snacks like fruit or chopped veggies, you might get stuck hearing, "Lighten up and have a cupcake for once."

Not only is this especially crappy for people who are struggling with disordered eating, it's pretty irritating for everyone else, too.

If you work with someone who does this regularly, it's okay to speak up and ask for it to stop! You could say:

- *"Let's avoid diet talk here—it's not good for anyone."*

- *"Do you realize that you comment on what I'm eating nearly every day?"*

- *"Hey, would you please stop commenting on what I eat? Thank you."*

- *"We all get so much pressure about what we eat. Let's not bring it into the office too."*

Most people who regularly comment on other people's food haven't stopped to consider how it might be received, so being direct about it can sometimes jolt them into realizing that they're not just making harmless conversation.

13. Coworker is pushing food on you

A variation of the coworker who takes an inordinate interest in what you eat is the coworker who's aggressive about pushing food on you—insisting that you need to have a slice of cake or at least a bite of the homemade doughnuts she brought in. A simple "No, thank you" should work, but with aggressive food pushers, that isn't always enough.

If you regularly have to fend off insistent attempts to get you to eat things you don't want, try saying this:

- *"No, thank you. I'm impressed with how well you cook, but I'm trying to be disciplined about what I eat. It can be tough when people push snacks on me, so I'd really appreciate it if you'd let me just say 'No, thanks.'"*

14. Coworker doesn't respond to your emails

If you work with someone who's unresponsive to emails, sometimes the best course of action is to give up on using email and instead talk in person or pick up the phone. That's annoying if you're an email person, but sometimes that's the only way you're going to get what you need.

That said, before entirely giving up on email, it can be worth asking the person directly if there's something you can do differently that would make it easier for her to respond to you:

- *"I've noticed that I often don't hear back from you about requests I send via email. Is there something you'd like me to do differently when I need something from you?"*

At a minimum, this will call the person's attention to the problem (and maybe shame her a bit, which isn't a bad thing in this situation). But it might also get you some helpful insight that you can use—for example, that she'll respond more quickly if you flag action items in the subject line, or that she's able to field emails more quickly in the mornings, or who knows what.

You can also try proposing a course of action that you'll take if you don't hear back by a certain time. This isn't practical in every case, but often it's fine to say:

- *"If I don't hear back from you by Thursday, I'll plan to do X so that we stay on schedule."*

Keep in mind that if you do this, you have to give the person a reasonable amount of time to respond (an hour isn't usually enough, for example). And of course, you can't do this in situations where you don't have the authority to move forward without the person's input—but in many cases it can help move something along.

15. Coworker doesn't give you enough time to respond to emails

Every office has that irritating coworker who shows up at your desk just minutes after emailing you to ask, "Did you read my email?" Or who follows up with an increasingly agitated message when they haven't heard back about a nonurgent email sent just a couple of hours ago. (Hopefully this irritating coworker isn't you. If it's you, you must repent and resolve to stop.)

If you have a coworker who does this, try this formula: "I've noticed you do X / It's a problem because of Y / Can you do Z instead? I promise it will get you what you need."

For example:

• *"Hey, I've noticed that you'll often come by to check if I received an email you just sent. I promise you that I will look at your emails and respond to them, but it really breaks my focus when you come over to check. When you've sent an email, can you give me some time to respond? Sometimes it may take me a few hours, or even longer if it's not time-sensitive, but I'm really vigilant about getting back to everyone."*

Or, if you don't want to get into all that, you can sometimes just retrain the person by sticking to this response when interrupted:

- *"Sorry, I'm on deadline, but I'll take a look at your email when I'm done."*

Obviously you shouldn't do this with your boss; we're talking peers and below here.

16. Coworker keeps coming in to work sick and contagious

If you have a coworker who keeps coming to work sick and spreading germs around, you probably want to scream, "Stay home, germ-monger!"

You probably shouldn't say it quite that way, but you can say something similar as long as (a) your office provides reasonably generous paid sick leave and/or (b) your coworker could work from home. (If neither of those things is the case, your coworker may not realistically be able to stay home.)

Here are some ways to word it:

- *"Would you be willing to work from home while you're sick? I tend to catch colds and flus easily, and I imagine others may be the same."*

- *"You must be miserable, and to be honest, I'm worried about catching it too. Can I take anything off your plate to make it easier for you to work from home or take sick leave?"*

- If you have the right rapport with the person: *"Dude, you are infecting the whole office. Go home!"*

17. Coworker keeps interrupting your conversations with others

If you have a coworker who always butts into your conversations—for example, answering questions you directed to other people or just showing up in a private conversation that you didn't intend him to be a part of—you probably feel awkward asking him to stop. Especially if you're in an open-plan office, it can be tough to navigate the etiquette around which conversations are private and which are open to everyone.

And frankly, if the conversation is a social one and you're having it in a fairly public area, it would be rude to insist on excluding someone who wanted to join in.

But if the conversation is work-related, you're allowed to set some boundaries. Here are some ways to do it:

- *"Actually, I really want to get Anna's input on this."*

- *"Thanks for the thoughts! For now I really want to talk to Anna about it, though, since she used to work on this project."*

- *"Oh, I'm talking to Anna about a work project—did you need one of us? We'll probably be about five more minutes."*

18. Coworker monopolizes meetings

People who act as if every meeting is a stage for their monologues—and who dominate the conversation with lengthy comments on everything that comes up, no matter how irrelevant—usually get away with it because no one wants to be the one to tell them to cut it out.

If you're the one running the meeting, you're in luck: You have the authority, and in fact the obligation, to redirect the conversation. You can rescue the meeting by being ready with statements like these:

- *"I want to be sure we get through all the items on the agenda, so let's move on to our next topic."*

- *"We only have forty-five minutes scheduled today, so I'm going to ask people to hold comments until the end unless they're crucial."*

- *"It's an interesting point, but it's taking us away from our agenda today, so let's table that for now and we can come back to it if we have time at the end."*

- *"I'd love to give others a chance to weigh in. Who else has thoughts on this?"*

If you're not running the meeting, your options are more limited, but you can still do your part to move the conversation along:

- *"I think we're getting away from the scope of our agenda today. Should we move back to the plan for the new office?"*

- *"It sounds like we're all in agreement about how to move forward. Should we get away from the exact details and move on to the other two items on the agenda?"*

- *"I just want to note the time—I know Ari had a couple of other items we need to discuss today and it might make sense to focus on those."*

19. Coworker is a know-it-all who tries to tell you how to do your work

If you work with someone who has an opinion on everything—and not just an opinion but the One True Answer—and loves to tell you how to do your job better, your best bet is to ignore the person as much as possible. You're not likely to reform a know-it-all, so you're better off with a goal of simply not letting it get to you.

That means being armed with responses like these:

- *"Thanks, I'll think about that."*

- *"I've got it covered, but thanks."*

- *"I feel good about how I'm handling this, but I'll let you know if I end up needing input."*

Keep it short and breezy and don't engage.

My coworker treats me like his assistant

A reader writes:

I work in a small office, seven people total. I love my job and I've always received glowing reviews from my boss, the general manager. However, this is a male-dominated office, with me and one other coworker the only women who work here.

Another coworker (let's call him Jim) refuses to learn our operating system, which includes all client data. He will walk up to my desk and interrupt whatever work I'm currently in the middle of to ask me to look up a customer and information about their service. He will even interrupt my lunch break (while I have headphones in) and ask me to look up client information. If he sees me on the phone with a client, he will instead walk over to the other woman in our office (let's call her Mandy) and ask her to look up information instead. He will even call Mandy or me with questions about clients when he is out of the office, at home, sitting in front of his company laptop!

Jim treats both of us as his assistants, although neither of our jobs is related to his. He will ask Mandy or me to prepare presentations for customers who neither of us have contact with. He's asked me to help him format his email signature or save a picture onto his desktop, and other things that are incredibly simple to do. All of these tasks he has the time to do, but he just doesn't want to do them.

Jim has worn a path in the carpet of our office, from his desk, to my desk, to Mandy's desk, and back. There's nothing he won't ask either of us to do, and it doesn't matter how busy we are. He's never asked any other coworkers for help, and I feel like he's asking Mandy and me because we're the women in the office.

How do I ask him to stop bothering me with tasks that he should know how to do?

He's continuing to do this because you and Mandy are inadvertently reinforcing the behavior by allowing it. Stop rewarding his behavior with help and answers, and retrain him to do this stuff himself or look elsewhere for answers.

Use responses like these:

- "Sorry, I'm on deadline. Try checking the manual."

- "I'm not sure. Have you asked Leo or Jose?"

- "Have you checked the database? That's the first place to look."

- "Sorry, I've got to get this finished before my lunch break ends."

- "You want me to prepare a presentation for your client? Sorry, I'm busy with X, Y, and Z. Kat, Leo, and Jose all do that for themselves, so maybe one of them can show you how they do it."

- "Sorry, I'm swamped right now."

- "What have you tried so far?"

- "Can't help! Sorry!"

- "Jose does fantastic presentations. Try checking with him."

- "I don't know anything about those customers—sorry!"

At some point, you could also consider just asking him head-on about what's going on. As in: "Hey, I'm curious about why you keep asking Mandy and me for help with these items, since we work in different areas than you. Have you tried asking Leo or Jose, since they do work so similar to yours?" Depending on his answer, you might follow up with: "Have you noticed that you only ask the women in the office for assistance?"

That said, before you do this, make sure that you and your manager are on the same page about what your role is. If there's any chance that Jim is treating you like his assistant because he's been told that it's appropriate to go to you with these things, you need to know that. Otherwise, you need to know that your manager will have your back if Jim complains.

20. Coworker keeps passive-aggressively cc'ing your manager on emails

It can be really annoying to have a coworker continually cc your manager on emails. It's hard not to interpret regular cc'ing of a higher-up as "I don't trust you to handle this correctly on your own" or "I think your boss needs to be aware of how incompetent you are."

If you're sure that your manager hasn't asked to be looped in and doesn't prefer it, you can speak up! For example:

- *"I've noticed that you're cc'ing Flora on most of your emails to me. Is there a reason you're looping her in?"*

- *"You actually don't need to cc Flora on this stuff. We try to keep these sorts of issues streamlined so that we don't inadvertently duplicate efforts. Can you start with me on this stuff, and then we can always loop her in if we need to?"*

If that doesn't work, your best bet is probably to stop worrying about it. Ideally your boss would tell her to cut it out, but if that's not happening, it's generally not worth pushing the issue—in part because pushing it after one or two conversations can make it seem that you're oddly invested in keeping your boss *out* of the loop.

21. Coworker keeps going over your head rather than bringing concerns to you directly

There are times when it would make sense for a coworker to go straight to your boss rather than first talking with you about a problem—for instance, if you're embezzling company funds or punching clients or something else that scores high on the list of Seriously Unacceptable Behavior. But in most cases, it's okay to ask a coworker to come talk with you directly first, so that you have a chance to resolve whatever the concern is:

- *"Yori told me that you passed along some concerns about X. In the future, can you bring input like that to me first so that I have a chance to hear your concerns directly from you and ask questions if I need to?"*

- *"Since I'm managing the X project, would you come directly to me if you have concerns about it? If we're not able*

to resolve them between ourselves and you feel it's impor-
tant enough to take to Yori at that point, of course you
should. But I'm hoping that you'll start with me so that I
have a chance to hear and respond to your concerns."

One big exception to this approach: If your coworker has
pointed out issues to you in the past and is now concerned
that there's a pattern, it actually *is* appropriate for him to escalate straight to your manager. Talking about a concerning
pattern is manager feedback stuff (and something that a peer
doesn't really have standing to address with you anyway).

22. Coworker keeps checking her phone or email while you're trying to meet with her

Whether and how to say something to a colleague who's at-
tached to her phone or email when you're trying to talk with
her really depends on hierarchy. Your approach should be
different depending on whether you're in a junior, senior, or
peer relationship to the person.
   If you're peers, try one of these:

• *"Should I give you a few minutes to take care of that?"*

• *"I think this will go more quickly if we can focus on it for*
  a few minutes. Is now good, or do you need to deal with
  your phone/email?"

• *"I know you're juggling a bunch of things and are having*
  to deal with stuff coming in on your phone/email. Do you
  think we can focus on this for a few minutes? I don't think
  we'll need long."

If the person is junior to you, you can be pretty direct about asking her to stop:

- *"Can you put that away while we're meeting, please?"*

But if the person is senior to you, you need to be more delicate in your approach. For example:

- *"It looks like you're busy! Should I come back?"*

Beyond that, though, it's usually a senior person's prerogative to decide to multitask during a meeting (especially if that senior person is your manager!). But if it becomes a pattern, you could try saying something like this:

- *"When you're on your phone for so much of our meeting time, it's tough for me to know if I should keep talking or wait for you to finish, or how much you're able to focus. I know you're really busy. Is there a different time we could schedule our meetings that might be better for you?"*

23. Your cubemate wears perfume you're allergic to

If you're sensitive to the fragrance a coworker wears—if it gives you headaches, makes it hard for you to breathe, or otherwise makes your office environment a physically uncomfortable one—you'll need to say something. Your interest in being able to work without physical discomfort trumps someone else's desire to smell like roses or patchouli or musk.

The key is to make it clear that you're not passing judgment on your coworker's fragrance or implying that she's doing something rude; the scent just happens to be one that triggers your allergies. For example:

- *"Your perfume is lovely, but it seems to be triggering my allergies and giving me headaches. I'm so sorry to ask, but would you be willing to leave it off at the office?"*

- *"I'm so sorry about this, but I'm highly allergic to some fragrances and your perfume seems to be setting off my allergies. I know this is a lot to ask, but would you be willing to help me out by not wearing it in the office?"*

24. You're being pressured to donate money toward a coworker's gift

Your coworker is getting married! Or retiring! Or having a baby! Or a birthday! And hurrah—you're being asked to contribute money to buy gifts for all of these occasions.

To some extent, chipping in small amounts of money for social occasions like these every now and then is part of working in an office with other people. It's a thing that happens.

But sometimes the practice goes horribly wrong, and people start getting pressured to donate constantly and/or to donate unreasonable amounts of money. If you're being pressured to donate more than you can afford or want to give, it's okay to speak up and say no. Here's how to say it:

- *"I'm sorry, it's not in my budget right now."*

- *"I'm stretched pretty thin right now, but I'd be glad to sign a card."*

- *"I can't contribute right now, but it's really nice of you to take the lead on organizing something for Callista."*

- *"I can donate five dollars, but my budget won't let me contribute more than that. If others feel the same, maybe we could buy a less expensive gift or just get a card?"*

25. You're being pressured to donate to a workplace charity drive you don't support

Workplaces generally mean well when they organize charity drives, but too often they forget that participation should be strictly voluntary and wind up inappropriately pressuring people to donate.

You aren't a cheapskate or a jerk if you don't want to contribute to a particular collection. Your money is yours, and you get to decide how to use it. But if you're on the receiving end of high-pressure tactics to get you to donate, try any of these:

- *"My budget won't allow me to contribute right now."*

- *"I already allocated my charity budget for the year."*

- *"It's a great cause, but I can't."*

- *"No, thank you."*

That said, if you're working in a culture where opting out will impact you professionally—which shouldn't be the case but sometimes is—then it might make sense to donate a few dollars and consider it the price you pay to make the pressure go away. Sometimes that's the sensible option, even if it grates on principle.

My coworker stole donations from a gift collection

A reader writes:
One of my coworkers collected donations for Boss's Day gifts for our project manager and assistant project manager. But over a month after the holiday, a gift had not been given. The person's excuse was that she kept forgetting. A lot of people kept asking her about it; I know I asked two times. Still, though, no gifts. We finally told the assistant project manager, and he went up to her and asked about the donations and where the gift for our project manager was. She made an excuse and said that she decided to save that money for a Christmas gift for them instead. Well, she never informed us of her change in plans. So a week later, she gives our manager a hand-made item she bought. This is not what we agreed on.

We don't know how much she collected for two gifts, but what I gave was way more than the one gift, so basically she kept a lot of money. I know we will never trust this person with money again. What should we do or can we do?

You should tell her clearly and firmly—preferably with the rest of the people who donated—that you want an accounting of how the money was spent, including a receipt, and that you want the remainder returned. If it helps to have specific language, I'd start by saying this: "It seems like there must be money left over from the gift purchase—can you show us the receipt for the final cost so we can figure out how to divide up and return the money that was left over?"

And unless she makes this right immediately after that, you should give your boss a heads-up about what happened, because stealing from coworkers is a serious thing.

26. Coworker keeps touching you and you're not into it

In theory, you probably know that you don't have to let yourself be touched by a coworker—that your right not to be touched takes precedence over the other person's interest in hugging you, rubbing your shoulders, or putting an arm around you. But in reality, it can be tough to tell someone "Quit touching me" without worrying that you're implying "I think you're a pervert" (which may or may not be what you really mean, and which you might reasonably worry would impact the working relationship). Because of that, a lot of people put up with unwanted touching.

But this doesn't have to be a super-awkward conversation that harms the relationship. As your opening salvo, try saying this:

- *"Oh, I'm not a toucher!"*

Say it cheerfully and briskly and then immediately move on to something work-related, and it's likely that the toucher will get the message and appreciate your handling of it.

However—and this is important—if the toucher turns this back on you and acts like you're the problem, or if the touching continues after this, then that person is a problem. At that point, you should stop worrying about introducing tension into the relationship. *He* is the one introducing that tension—by ignoring your clearly stated wishes—and at that point you should have no qualms about escalating. Escalating might mean icily delivering this:

- *"As I said, please don't touch me."*

Or it might mean pulling in someone above you, depending on the circumstances.

(And of course, we're talking here about nonsexual touching. If it's sexual, skip straight to "Get your hands off me" and report that crap.)

27. Turning down a coworker who asks you out

Rejecting a coworker who asks you out can be a lot more awkward than rejecting someone outside of work, because you're going to continue to see each other every day.

The best thing to do is to be straightforward . . . and as normal as possible afterward. Most people will take their cues from you, so if you act like everything is still fine and normal, it's likely to ease much of the other person's awkwardness. On the other hand, if you're acting uncomfortable, the other person is likely to respond in kind.

As for what to say, try any of these:

- *"Thank you, but I'd rather keep things between us professional."*

- *"Thank you for the invitation. I'm not interested in dating, but I enjoy working with you."*

- *"Thank you, but I don't date coworkers."* (This one has the potential for awkwardness if you do later end up dating a different coworker. You're allowed to change your mind, of course, but factor that in if you choose it.)

28. Coworker asks you to keep a secret from your boss that you're uncomfortable keeping

If your coworker asks you to keep a secret from your boss, it might be no big deal to agree (if the secret is, say, "I think this strategy is silly" or "I really just needed a day off for my mental health"). But sometimes agreeing would put you in a really uncomfortable or even untenable situation (like if your coworker said "I'm stealing from the company" or "I'm going to keep asking out that intern who keeps saying no").

If you find yourself in possession of knowledge that you feel ethically required to share, usually the best thing to do is to be honest about that. You can say it this way:

- *"I'm in a difficult position here. This is the kind of thing I'm obligated to bring to Cecily's attention if I know about it. I want to be transparent with you that I feel I have to share this with her. I'm sorry that's the case—I know you intended to confide in me. But I hope you can see why it puts me in a tough spot. Would you prefer to talk to her about it yourself?"*

29. Coworkers invite you to frequent social events that you don't want to attend

If you work with a group of people who often socialize together outside of work, it can feel awkward to keep turning down invitation after invitation. You don't want your coworkers to think you don't like them, but you also might prefer to keep a boundary between your work life and your social life.

If that's the case, try one of these responses:

- *"Hey, I really appreciate your inviting me to this stuff. I usually have other plans in the evenings / I tend to go straight home after work / I'm not one for happy hours, but thank you for thinking of me. I hope you all have a great time there!"*

- *"You're so nice to invite me to these things. I tend to like to have a separation between work and the rest of my life, so I generally won't take you up on these invitations, but I really appreciate your including me in them."*

30. Setting boundaries with a coworker who wants more of a friendship than you do

When a coworker wants a closer friendship than you'd prefer—like hanging out outside of work, calling you in the evenings, or otherwise moving the relationship from friendly coworkers to real-life friends—declining politely is tricky. When someone you know socially wants a closer relationship than you do, it's easier to set boundaries and limit the amount of interaction that you have. But with a coworker, you're likely to have regular interaction whether you want to or not, and that makes most of the usual signals for "I don't like you *that way*" much harder to send.

That leaves you with two options: You can rely on hints and cues, or you can be direct.

Relying on hints and cues sounds like a cop-out, but in this context it can be kinder if it gets the message across without hurting the person's feelings. The key—and it is a very, very important key—is that if you see that hints and cues aren't working, you switch tactics.

But you can start with hints and cues and see if that solves the problem:

- *"My schedule is packed right now, so I'm not able to hang out outside of work."*

- *"I'm not able to email much during the day because I'm usually on deadline."*

- *"Sorry, I'm swamped right now and can't really talk."*

- *"I have a lot of work right now, so I can't be social."*

But if you do that a handful of times and your coworker is still pushing you to come to happy hour every night, spend an hour chatting with him at work, and so forth, then it's kinder to be more direct:

- *"I like going to happy hour sometimes, but for me it's a once-every-few-months thing, and I'm not up for it more often than that."*

- *"I got your message asking me to hang out last weekend. To be honest, I like to keep a separation between my work life and my personal life, so I don't do much socializing with coworkers. But that art show you were going to sounds really cool, and I hope you had a great time!"*

Be warm and cheerful in your tone, and you'll probably be able to successfully assert and maintain the boundaries you want.

My coworker wants us to call her boyfriend her "master"

A reader writes:

An employee, "Sally," started at our workplace about a year and a half ago. She's not my subordinate, but she is the subordinate of a peer of mine and works frequently with my subordinates. A few months later she got a new boyfriend, "Peter." (I found out about this through normal water-cooler-type conversation.)

After she'd been with the company a few more months, she invited her boyfriend to our holiday party. (This is totally normal in our workplace.) Everything there seemed fine as well, although at one point Peter asked Sally to get him a drink, to which she replied "Yes, master!" in a very I Dream of Jeannie kind of way. We all laughed it off as a joke, and it didn't come up again.

. . . until it did. We had an early summer party in late

May which Sally and Peter both attended. At this party, there was a good deal more of Peter ordering Sally around and Sally calling him "master": He sent her to fetch drinks and hot dogs, he told her to find a place for them to sit, etc., to which she replied consistently "Yes, master." It made a number of people, myself included, clearly uncomfortable, but there was nothing objectively abusive about it (he never yelled at her or threatened her), and her immediate supervisor and her supervisor's supervisor weren't there, and so no one said anything (perhaps incorrectly?).

After the party, at the office, I overheard a conversation in which one of her coworker-friends was like, "So, uh, what's up with the master thing?" and she explained that she was in a 24/7 dominant/submissive relationship, and he wasn't her boyfriend or her S.O. or her partner, he was her "master," and he needed to be referred to as such. Her coworker was clearly flummoxed and didn't have much response to that.

Later, I heard her correct someone who referred to her boyfriend as her partner, saying that he wasn't her partner, he was her master, and should be referred to using his appropriate title. She compared it to gay rights, saying that if she was a man, they wouldn't erase her relationship by referring to "Peter" as "Patricia," and so they shouldn't erase the D/s relationship by calling him a partner instead of a master. It's pretty clear that her coworkers aren't comfortable asking "Will your master be at the end-of-summer barbecue?" or "Did you and your master do anything fun this weekend?," though, and thus have just stopped referring to Peter at all.

Her direct boss, my colleague, is baffled as to how to sensitively address this issue. My instinct is that there's a very big difference between insisting that colleagues

acknowledge that you're in a gay relationship and insist-
ing that they refer to your partner as your "master," and
that it borders on involving other nonconsenting parties
in your relationship . . . but I can't really articulate why. For
what it's worth, I am a bisexual woman, and our office has
a number of gay/lesbian, trans, and poly individuals, so
it's not an issue of being against nontraditional relation-
ships. It just seems to be very important to Sally that Peter
be referred to as her "master," and it seems equally clear
that her coworkers find this intensely uncomfortable.

Help! How can I advise my colleague? What's reason-
able in this situation?

Whoa. Yeah, your coworkers definitely don't need to refer to Peter as Sally's "master," and she's wildly out of line to request or expect it.

What Sally is asking for is indeed akin to involving nonconsenting parties in their sex life and in their relationship. Even if she wanted to argue that the term isn't a sexual one (which is a bit of a stretch), she's still insisting that people participate in a dynamic of her relationship with Peter that they haven't signed up to be a part of.

That may become more intuitive if you consider that there isn't actually any need here for a label more specific than "partner" (or, you know, even just "Peter"). "Partner" is a conveniently generic term that covers a whole spectrum of possibilities—boyfriend, girlfriend, spouse, long-term companion, asexual mate, and so forth. There's no need to use a term that describes the dynamic between them so specifically. After all, imagine if you had a coworker who insisted that people identify her partner as her "lover." It's too much information, it's not needed, and it's understandably going to make people uncomfortable. (The "lover" comparison works particularly nicely, since anyone insisting on it would come across as just as self-involved as Sally is here. And to be clear, Sally's behavior *is* self-involved; making a point of describing the inner workings of your relationship to colleagues and insisting that they use very specific, sexually charged language to describe it when a more generic term would do perfectly well is very much the province of people who are indulging their own urges at the expense of consideration for others.)

And really, "partner" *should* cover it. It might be an unequal partnership, but it's still a partnership.

That's why refusing to refer to Peter as Sally's "master" isn't at all equivalent to refusing to acknowledge gay couples or calling someone who identifies as a man by a woman's name. You're not refusing to recognize the relationship's validity; in fact, by referring to Peter as your coworker's partner, you're inherently recognizing the relationship's validity. No one is being erased.

But Sally is asking for more than that: She's asking you to get involved in and play along with a specific dynamic of their relationship. It's entirely reasonable to decline to do that. Whatever she and Peter agree to do together is all well and good, but you and your coworkers don't need to participate in it.

And the fact that this is happening at work, as opposed to just in a social situation, gives this a whole additional layer of weirdness and discomfort. It would be odd enough if Sally were just doing this socially, but it's infinitely weirder and more disturbing that she's making it a Thing at work—where people normally have stronger boundaries than this, where she has something of a captive audience, and where people feel pressure not to cause tension in their relationships with her.

So, should her boss—your friend—say something to

her about it? Probably, especially if it's making people uncomfortable, as of course it is. If Sally pushes back with the gay rights comparison again, her manager can point out that everyone is happy to acknowledge her relationship with Peter, but they're going to use the term "partner" as they do with everyone else—gay, straight, poly, or any other relationship category.

31. Explaining that you don't friend coworkers on social media

People have all sorts of preferences for whether and how they connect with coworkers on social media. Some people will connect on LinkedIn but not on Facebook because they want to preserve boundaries between work and the rest of their life, while others are perfectly comfortable connecting anywhere. Either choice is legitimate, but if you're in the first group, you may occasionally run into a coworker who wants to know why you haven't accepted her Facebook friend request.

One option, of course, is to accept the friend request and then adjust your privacy settings so that no one from work can see your posts. But if you'd rather not do that, try one of these:

- *"Oh, I'm old-fashioned about Facebook. It's been drilled into me to keep professional and personal stuff separate. Let's connect if one of us moves to another company, though!"*

- *"I'm hardly ever on Facebook anymore. I really just use it to see photos of my nieces and nephews. Let's connect on LinkedIn, though!"*

(These options work for your boss, too, not just peers!)

32. Asking a coworker to stop texting you outside work hours

If a coworker is blowing up your phone with texts when you're not even at work and you want it to stop, here are two ways to say it:

- *"Getting texts in the evening is making it hard for me to disconnect from work. Would you hold these until the workday? I'd really appreciate it!"*

- *"I try to unplug from work once I'm home at night. If you need to send me something after work hours, would you send it to my email rather than texting? That way I'll see it when I'm back in work mode. Thank you!"*

33. Coworker is trying to get you to take sides in a dispute and you don't want to be involved

People disagree about things at work, and that's normal. But you're not obligated to take sides in a dispute that you have no particular stake in. Most coworkers will respect that stance, but if a coworker pressures you to take sides in a disagreement that you'd prefer to stay out of, here are some things you can say:

- *"My working relationship with each of you is important to me, so I'm sitting this one out."*

- *"I can see both sides. I'd prefer to stay out of it, though. Thanks for respecting that."*

- *"I can see that you're upset, and I'm sorry this is happening. I have to work with both of you, though, so I can't take sides."*

- *"That sounds really tough, but I don't think I'm the right person to weigh in here. I'm sorry I can't help."*

34. You accidentally trash-talked someone who was cc'd on an email

Everyone warns about this happening, and yet somehow you never think it will happen to you . . . until the moment you feel the gut punch of realizing you just sent an email complaining about a coworker to that very coworker.

What to do? Take responsibility and apologize. It's going to be awkward for both of you, but it's the right thing to do and it's going to be less awkward than letting it fester for weeks or months. For example:

- *"I need to apologize to you for the email I just sent. My comment was unkind and I'm embarrassed by it. I'm very sorry for what I said."*

If your trash-talking was rooted in a legitimate work concern that you haven't addressed with the person directly, this might be the time to suck it up and do that. For example:

- *"I need to apologize to you for the email I sent earlier today. I made an unkind comment about how you handled the X project. I was blowing off steam, but it's no excuse. The reality is, I was frustrated by how late the assignment came to me and I wished I'd had more advance notice. But I*

*should have talked with you directly about that, not com-
plained to someone else."*

35. You got drunk at the company holiday party

So, you drank too much at a company event. Maybe you had
an empty stomach and misjudged what you could handle, or
maybe your nerves got the better of you, or maybe you just
threw caution to the wind and overindulged. Whatever the
reason, in addition to your splitting headache and the spin-
ning room, you're now facing the terrible realization that
your coworkers saw you dancing on tables / slurring your
words / ranting drunkenly like a loon. (Hey, it could be
worse. I once received a letter from someone who got drunk
at the company holiday party and punched his boss. Hopefully you didn't do that.)

If you embarrassed yourself, the best thing to do is to confront the situation head-on: Acknowledge to the people you
had the most interaction with (as well as your boss if she
observed you) that you had too much to drink, say that you'll
exercise more control in the future, and—if you think you
made anyone uncomfortable—apologize. For example:

- *"I'm mortified about my behavior at the party on Friday. I
  didn't realize that I'd had too much to drink, but clearly I
  did. I'm so sorry if I made you or anyone else uncomfortable, and I won't be drinking at company events in the
  future."*

Also, if there's an easy explanation for what happened, like
that you hadn't realized you were drinking on an empty

stomach, it can be smart to mention that, too, so people have some context for what happened.

Coworker keeps burping loudly

A reader writes:

My department is pretty quiet. Most of the floor is waist-high cubes (i.e., no privacy), so we're all fairly considerate of each other: earbuds for music, taking personal calls out to the stairwell, etc.

There's a line of small offices—with doors—down one side of the room. Our new IT help-desk guy has been installed in one of the offices. In most ways he's a huge improvement over the last couple of help-deskers we've had: reasonably friendly, seems to know what he's doing, gets things done.

The problem? He belches. Daily. Horrid, long, loud, disgusting belches. Even with his office door closed, some days it's downright nauseating.

I don't know how to approach him about it. His supervisor is in a different building altogether. Our HR "department" is one overworked person who mostly deals with hiring and benefits. I don't want to be a jerk about it, but it's getting disruptive and something's got to change. Any ideas?

It's possible that it's a medical problem, in which case there likely isn't anything that he can do about it. But it might not be medical at all, and you don't need to assume that it is without first talking to him. I'd say it this way: "Hey, I don't know if you realize that when you burp, we can hear it out here. It's pretty distracting! Anything you can do to control it or at least keep it quieter?"

36. Coworker makes bigoted remarks

If you have a coworker who makes racist, homophobic, or otherwise bigoted remarks, there are lots of work-appropriate ways to say "That's unwelcome and I don't want to hear it." Here are some options you can try:

- *"I hope you're not saying that because you think I agree with you."*

- *"I find that really offensive. Please don't say that sort of thing around me."*

- *"I feel very differently about this subject than you do, and I don't want to hear this kind of thing at work. Please stop."*

- *"Comments like that are offensive to most people and unwelcome at work. I don't want to hear comments like that."*

If your bigot responds by saying the comments aren't that bad, that you're being too sensitive, or, really, anything other than agreeing to stop, say this:

- *"Again, I'm telling you that those comments are unwelcome here. And they expose the company to legal liability under federal harassment laws, so I really need you to stop."*

If that doesn't work, your next step should be to talk to your boss or HR, because your coworker really is creating legal liability for your company, and they'll want to stop it. (Frankly, you'd be justified in going directly to HR if you want to, particularly if the remarks are way over the line. But in many cases HR will ask you whether you asked the person to stop, and it's helpful to be able to say yes.)

37. Coworker subjects you to constant political talk

In social situations, you can (usually) avoid boors who try to force you to listen to unwelcome political rants. At work, it's often much harder since you're a captive audience—and, on top of that, you have the pressure of not wanting to add tension into a working relationship.

But that doesn't mean that you're stuck engaging in political discussions against your will. You just need to be willing to ask—politely but assertively—for it to stop. For example:

- *"I'd rather not discuss politics at work. Thanks for understanding!"*

- *"Aggh, I'm so sick of politics. Let's discuss something else."*

- *"I have a rule that I don't discuss politics at work. But did you hear there's going to be a doughnut truck in the parking lot tomorrow morning?"*

If the person continues after that, then you escalate in firmness:

- *"I'm banning political discussions between us—seriously, please stop."*

- *"I'm not willing to discuss this with you. Please stop. Anyway, can you tell me the status of the new product flyer?"*

If direct requests don't work, then pointedly changing the subject (especially to something work-related) or even finding a reason to leave the room (like grabbing something from the printer or heading to the kitchen) will usually short-circuit the boor.

38. Responding to unwelcome religious talk

If your coworker asks whether you've been saved, or insists on knowing the details of your religious faith (or lack thereof), or otherwise tries to pull you into a religious conversation that you'd prefer not to have at work, the best thing you can do is to be direct:

- *"I prefer not to discuss religion at work. Thanks for understanding!"*

A big advantage to this approach is that it will be immediately clear whether the person is going to be respectful of you or not. A reasonable person, upon hearing this, will back off immediately. An unreasonable person will not.

If you're dealing with an unreasonable person who keeps imposing religious talk on you after you've told him to stop, at that point you should talk to your manager or HR, since in the United States, employers have a legal obligation to ensure that employees aren't subjected to religious harassment. When escalating it, you'd use these words:

- *"I've asked Logan to stop discussing religion with me, but he has insisted on continuing. Can you please ensure that I'm able to work without religious harassment?"*

39. Older coworker keeps trying to parent you

If you're a youngish person in the work world, you may run into an older colleague whose interactions with you feel more like a parent/child dynamic than a normal coworker dynamic. Sometimes this shows up as an overly familiar interest in your health, your dates, your diet, or even whether you've dressed appropriately for the weather.

If the comments are pretty mild, you might choose to just let them go or reply with a dry "Thanks, I've got it." But if the comments are frequent or you feel that they're undermining your ability to be taken seriously at work, speak up! For example:

Coworker: *"You're so adorable, and I'd love to see you find the right man. I think if you took more care with your hair and your clothes, you'd have men lining up."*

You: *"I'd rather not discuss my appearance or my dating life at work. Thanks!"* (If it makes it easier for you to say, you can begin with *"I know it comes from a kind place, but . . ."*)

Coworker: *"Don't forget a warm jacket—it's cold outside!"*

You: *"You've reminded me a few times, and I promise you I'm able to take care of that myself! I wouldn't bring it up ex-*

cept I've noticed you don't remind anyone but me, and I wouldn't want anyone thinking I'm less self-sufficient than anyone else here. Thanks for understanding."

Coworker: "That meeting on health insurance today was probably pretty overwhelming! Why don't I talk you through it?"

You: "I'm not sure if you realize how differently you treat me than the rest of our colleagues. I'm assuming it's because I'm younger, so this is me asking you to treat me the way you would any other colleague, rather than like a young person who needs your assistance."

40. Coworker keeps asking you for rides to or from work

I get a surprising number of letters at Ask a Manager from people whose coworkers won't stop asking for car rides! Often this is because the person willingly offered once or twice, but doesn't want to be the colleague's regular mode of transportation.

Frustratingly, the more you've said yes, the harder it can feel to say no. But you can reclaim your private time in your car if you want to! The easiest way to get out of being your coworker's chauffeur is by having other obligations that the rides will interfere with:

- "I won't be able to drive you anymore because I'm starting to do more things after work that take me in a different direction."

- "I'm going to start dropping my spouse off in the mornings so I can't pick you up anymore."

- *"I've been cutting it too close on some after-work commitments, so I won't be able to drive you anymore."*

Frankly, it's also okay to just explain that you value the alone time, if you're comfortable saying that:

- *"I'm finding that I really need alone time before/after work to recharge so I'm not exhausted later in the day. Thanks for understanding!"*

Keep in mind that if your coworker has been depending on you for rides regularly, it might be kind to give an advance heads-up a week or so before you want to change the routine, so that the person has time to make other arrangements.

41. You got a promotion that your coworker wanted

As excited as you might be about your new promotion, it can be tricky knowing what to say to a coworker who wanted the job herself. Rather than staying silent out of discomfort, addressing it head-on and saying something kind will often defuse some of the awkwardness:

- *"I know you were interested in the job too. I want to say that I think you're really talented and I know you would have done a good job."*

42. Coworker is rude to you (or otherwise a jerk)

If a coworker is a jerk to you—repeatedly rude, dismissive, or otherwise disrespectful—sometimes calling out the behavior calmly and kindly can make the person realize she's out of line and that you're not going to just lie down and take it.

I used almost this exact wording once when talking to a coworker who was quick to get frustrated and throw snark around:

- *"I like working with you, but I don't know if you realize how you talk to me sometimes. You can come across like you don't want to listen to what I have to say or you don't value my opinions. It can make working together pretty tricky."*

Another option:

- *"It sounds like you're frustrated, and I know this is aggravating. But you're using a pretty aggressive tone here that's making it hard to sort through this."*

You may not even need to say that much. Sometimes—especially in the face of open rudeness—it can be just as effective to give the person a pointed (or even disappointed) look and say something like:

- *"Wow, I hope you didn't mean that the way it sounded."*

- *"Whoa. What's going on?"*

- *"Where did that come from?"*

43. Coworker took credit for your idea

If your coworker takes credit for your ideas, don't stand by helplessly. Speak up and tell him that you want him to stop.

It's possible that he doesn't realize he's doing this, in which case pointing it out should be the nudge he needs. And if it's intentional, being called out on it should make it harder for him to do in the future.

- If it happens once: *"Hey, the idea you shared with Lillian earlier is the one I suggested in our meeting yesterday. I'm sure you didn't mean to imply it was yours, but going forward, can you make sure to attribute stuff like that to the person it came from, so that Lillian knows how we're all contributing?"*

- If it's a pattern: *"I've noticed that when I mention ideas to you, you'll often present them to Lillian without noting that they came from me. I want her to know what I'm contributing, so going forward, would you let me share my ideas with her myself?"*

- And if you see it happening in the moment, jump in and take the lead in the conversation: *"That's actually the idea I was explaining to Jaime before this meeting. My thinking about it is . . ."*

44. Coworker seems upset with you but you don't know why

If a coworker who's previously been friendly suddenly seems upset with you and you're not sure why, you have two options: Ignore it or say something.

Sometimes the right move can simply be to ignore it, give the person her space, and carry on cheerfully and professionally—particularly at work, where you might not want to get into a big discussion about emotions. And often this approach lets the person work things out internally in her own time.

But there are other times where you might want to ask what's going on, especially if you think you might have hurt or offended your colleague in some way. In that case, try one of these:

- *"I get the sense that I may have done something to upset you. If so, I'd want to try to make it right."*

- *"I've noticed we're not talking the way we used to. Have I done something to upset you?"*

- *"I'm afraid I may have inadvertently done something that upset you. If so, I'm really sorry about that! Can we clear the air?"*

45. You're not inviting your coworkers to your wedding

If you talk at all to your coworkers about your life, they're likely to know about it when you're getting married. And because lots of people like to talk about weddings, it can be easy to share so many details about your plans that it can then feel awkward to say, "Oh, but you're not invited."

Know that you're not obligated to invite coworkers to your wedding. If you want to, great! But if you don't, it's okay to say something like:

- *"We're keeping it small so we can't invite coworkers, unfortunately."*

- *"We've got big families so we're really limited on nonfamily invitations, unfortunately."*

- *"I wish we could invite everyone here, but we've got restrictions from the venue."*

The idea is to offer up an explanation that isn't "We don't like you enough." Most people understand that couples getting married face some restrictions on how many people they can invite, so if you put it in those terms, you should be able to avoid hard feelings.

I accidentally hugged the CEO

A reader writes:

Today as I was arriving at work, I got to the door of the building just before the CEO. I was holding the door for him, and he reached over me—I assume to take the door and hold it open for me. I'm a woman, and I don't know... chivalry? Anyway, my brain interpreted this as him going in for a hug. The reflex to hug back came quicker than the realization that greeting coworkers with a hug in the morning is not something people do. We both just pretended it hadn't happened and made small talk as we walked toward the elevator.

How embarrassed should I be about this? Is continuing to pretend it never happened a valid option for handling it going forward?

I'm friendly with him, but we don't really know each other well. He was involved in hiring me for a fairly junior position I've been in for six months, and a few months ago we had a running joke that's since died out, but we don't work together day to day at all. Possibly also relevant: It's a very laid-back company, a jeans-and-T-shirt kind of place.

Oh, this is totally something that would happen to me, and then I would feel burning mortification for days.

Ideally you would have made a joke about it in the moment ("OMG, I don't know where that came from; I'm on autopilot this morning") and laughed it off together.

But of course handling it well in the moment isn't

easy, especially when you're consumed by wondering "What the hell did I just do?" So you could do what I do when I'm dwelling on something with embarrassment later: Say something about it now. It means having to deal with the additional awkwardness of having a conversation about it, but I'm always so much happier to have corrected whatever mistaken impression I'm worried about (and I actually think people can find stuff like this endearing if you do it with the right amount of humor and self-deprecation).

So, the next time I saw him I'd say something like, "Um, I think I may have hugged you in the elevator the other morning. I was in a morning fog and I have no idea how that happened. I've been mortified ever since, so I felt I had to say something about it." I would then immediately feel ten times better, because even though we would now have had *two* awkward interactions, it would be worth the price to let him know I wasn't just randomly hugging him.

You may not feel that way, though! If doing that sounds unbearable to you, you might prefer to just let it go and use it as an embarrassing story to entertain others with. (And if your company was the sort where you rarely encountered him, it might make more sense to go that route anyway.)

And hell, maybe tell yourself that *he's* mortified because he thinks that you think he initiated a hug and that you felt pressured to go along with it.

46. When a coworker loses a loved one

A lot of people struggle with what to say to someone who has just experienced a devastating loss—they feel they have to come up with just the right comforting words, or they worry that mentioning the death will somehow remind the person of it (when in reality there's no danger that they've forgotten about it).

Luckily, etiquette has supplied the right words to use in this situation. You don't need to go searching for something creative (and in fact, doing that can backfire pretty terribly if you get it wrong). Stick to this formula: *I'm so sorry to hear of your loss / You're in my thoughts.*

- *"I was so sorry to hear about your mom. What a terrible loss. I wanted to let you know that I'm thinking of you and your family."*

You can say this in person if you'd like, but you can also put it in a card or even in an email. A surprising number of people don't say anything at all in this situation (out of discomfort, no doubt), and most grieving people are grateful for those who do acknowledge their loss.

47. Sharing difficult personal news with coworkers

Sharing difficult personal news at work—like that you've split up with a spouse or been diagnosed with a serious illness—can be tricky. You might not want to invite conversation about a painful topic or deal with the weird ways that some people react to bad news.

Assuming that you want to keep things low-key at work, the best approach here is to be fairly matter-of-fact. For example, if someone asks about your spouse, you might simply say, "Actually, Xavier and I are splitting up." Your coworker will then presumably express concern and sadness, and you can then say, "Thank you. It's a tough time, but we're getting through it," or "We're both doing okay"—something that assures people that you are in fact carrying on (and that they don't need to comfort you, if you don't want that).

Many people will feel inconsiderate if they don't inquire about what happened or how you're doing, so it can be important to make it explicitly clear if you prefer they not ask. Most people will understand that responses like "I'm doing fine and staying focused on work" signal "Let's not talk about it." But for people who don't get the hint, you can be more direct: "It's not something I want to get into at work, but I'm doing fine." (Even if you're not actually doing fine, this is the way to go if you want to ward off further conversation.)

Another option is to enlist someone else to share the news for you. That person could say something like, "Chloe called off her engagement. She's doing fine, but she would appreciate people not asking her about it."

48. Letting your coworkers know you're resigning when you're not yet ready to say where you're going

When you quit your job, it's likely that your coworkers will ask what you'll be doing next. Usually people are comfortable answering that question, but occasionally you might have a reason not to share where you're going. For example, you may have taken a new job with a competitor, or maybe your workplace is so dysfunctional that you don't trust your boss not to bad-mouth you to your new employer.

But because it's such a common thing to discuss, it can come across as weirdly chilly to refuse to say where you're going. You're better off giving a vague answer than an explicit refusal to share the information. For example, you could say:

- *"It's a small company in a different field. I'll be doing similar work to what I've done here, though."*

If pressed beyond that, you can say:

- *"I'm not ready to give details yet, but once everything's finalized, I'll let people know."*

49. What to say to a coworker who just got fired

People who have been fired will tell you that one of the weirdest parts of the experience is how many coworkers never reach out to them to say goodbye, in some cases even people they worked closely with for years.

It happens, of course, because people feel awkward and don't know what to say. If you're struggling with that, a good framework to use is the same one that you'd use with someone who left voluntarily. For example:

- *"I'm sorry to no longer be working with you! I've really valued you as a coworker, and I hope we can stay in touch. Please let me know if there's anything I can do to be helpful as you look for your next role."*

It's also kind to mention specific things you valued about working with him, especially since he may be feeling really down and would appreciate being reminded of his value. For example:

- *"I've learned so much by watching you handle difficult clients, and I really admire your ability to stay calm and thoughtful in the face of what's sometimes been chaos."*

It's also okay to say something empathetic about the firing itself, like "I'm sorry this happened." But generally you should avoid saying things like "I don't know what your manager was thinking" or "They're crazy to let you go," since in most cases you probably won't know the details of what happened (and firing decisions that are hard to understand from the outside often make a lot more sense when you're privy to all the details).

50. You're not comfortable being a reference for a coworker

If a coworker asks you to be a reference and you don't think you could give her a particularly good review, you have a few options for declining (none of them without awkwardness, I'm sorry to say):

- Be honest: *"I don't think I'm the right person, unfortunately, because of the struggles with X and Y when we worked together. I also know those may not be issues at other jobs, but it means I can't be a really strong reference. I'm sorry I can't help with this!"*

- Explain that you can't really characterize her work since you didn't manage her: *"I don't think I'd be a great refer-*

ence since I wasn't in a position to really see your work the way a manager would."

- Attribute it to the friendship, if there is one: *"I'm not comfortable giving references for friends, since I know that it biases me and can potentially harm my credibility, which could hurt you with the reference checker."*

- Be vague: *"Hmm, I don't think I'd be the best person for that. I'm sorry!"* or *"I'd love to help you in some other way, but I don't think I'd be the right reference."* (With these, you'll need to be prepared for the coworker to ask why. If she does, you could then use one of the other options on this list—but not everyone will push back and ask why, so it's possible this could get you off the hook.)

Can I have these conversations through email?

Most of the conversations in this book are intended to take place face-to-face—or in some cases, over the phone (for example, if you work in a different location than the person you're talking with). For the most part, they aren't ideal for email. Believe me, that pains me to say, because I'd conduct my whole life over email if I could. But when you're raising potentially sensitive or awkward topics, email has real disadvantages: You can't convey tone nearly as precisely as you can in person, and you can't get an immediate sense of the other person's reaction and adjust your approach if need be.

In fact, if you're dreading the conversation or it feels uncomfortable to you, that's an indication that the conversation is sufficiently delicate, emotionally charged, or ripe for misinterpretation that the odds of success are far higher if you talk in person. In those cases, you'll likely need a back-and-forth discussion rather than just one-way message delivery, and you'll want to have maximum control over your tone.

But if you do end up using email, keep these guidelines in mind:

- **Be brief.** Don't send someone paragraphs upon paragraphs of text—and that's especially important when something is highly charged, since a long email in that context is likely to come across as a rant.

- **Read your email over for tone before you send it.** Could it be misread as angry, brusque, or cold? What if the recipient already thought you might not like her? If so, sometimes just changing a few words can soften the tone. It seems silly, but look at the difference between these two emails:

Fergus,

Please come by my office to talk about how yesterday's launch went.

Jane

Hi, Fergus!

When you have a few minutes, I'd love to talk about how yesterday's launch went. Will you swing by this afternoon when you're free?

Thanks,

Jane

- **Pay attention to the communication norms of your particular office and calibrate yourself accordingly.** Some offices use email for everything. Others use email only for very straightforward work discussions and move to in-person conversations for everything else. In some offices, very concise, even terse emails are the norm. In others, you'll come across as overly brusque if you don't include more filler. Figuring out and adhering to the norms of your office will increase the chances that your message will be received well.

- **Be ready to switch mediums if email isn't getting you what you want.** Don't commit to email so wholeheartedly that you miss cues that you need to try a different medium. If the conversation is becoming heated or the other person seems annoyed, or if you repeatedly find yourself having to type out long paragraphs of text in reply, that's a sign that you need to pick up the phone or talk in person. And if you've sent a couple of emails to someone and haven't heard back, *email isn't working* and you need to try a different method.

CHAPTER 3

Conversations When You're the Boss

Here's the thing about being the boss: You have real power, which means that if there's a problem, it's very likely that you have the ability to fix it. You don't need to rely on cajoling or persuading people to do something differently. You have the authority—and in many cases the obligation—to be straightforward about what you need and to hold people accountable to whatever expectations you set for them.

That doesn't mean that you should be a jerk, of course. In fact, it's the opposite of that: Because you have authority and thus a great deal of control over people's livelihoods, you have an obligation to be kind and compassionate. But you need to do that while still setting a high bar for what you need and expect from your staff.

The hard part, of course, is figuring out how to balance all of that. Too often, in a quest to be kind, managers will soften their approach so much that their message is lost. But that ends up not being kind at all, if it denies an employee the chance to hear what he or she needs to do to excel at work (and in some cases to stay employed). And on the other end of the spectrum, some managers are so focused on the bottom line that they forget that they're dealing with humans, and that humans tend not to respond well to being treated like automatons.

It can be hard to find the sweet spot between those two extremes, so it's not surprising that many managers struggle to do it. But remembering these four principles can help you get there:

- **The kindest thing you can do for your staff members is to be really clear with them.** You're going to have to have tough conversations as a manager—it's part of the job. You might be tempted to put off a difficult conversation or to soften the message. You can't. You will do people a disservice if you're anything other than straightforward, particularly when there are aspects of their performance that you need them to change. If you hesitate to have tough conversations or if you sugarcoat the message, you make it more likely that people will continue frustrating or disappointing you, and that can have real consequences for them—such as impacting their future raises, promotions, project assignments, reputation, and even tenure in the job. You owe them directness and honesty.

- **Your tone matters . . . *a lot.*** Tone is important with any potentially awkward or sensitive conversation, but it's especially true when you're the boss. Your tone can determine whether someone walks away thinking "That was hard to hear, but I'm glad we talked" or "That was horrible and I want to go hide in the bathroom the rest of the day." The *words* you use need to be clear and direct, but your *tone* can still be kind and compassionate.

- **Talk, don't scold.** When something goes wrong, managers, and especially newer managers, often think that they need to come down hard on employees. But the vast majority of the time, you don't. Simply talking over what happened, why, and how you'll avoid it in the future is a form of accountability, and it's often all you need to get things back on track, particularly with conscientious employees. "What happened?" and "What's going on?" are handy questions that are often all you need to make the point that you're concerned about something. (Certainly if you find yourself having multiple "What happened?" conversations with the same person, you have a more serious issue on your hands . . . but you can start off with a lighter touch.)

- **With particularly tough or tricky conversations, try writing out talking points and practicing them beforehand.** Planning ahead of time can help structure your thoughts and ensure that you hit the key points. And while practicing out loud might feel silly, it can be hugely useful in helping you stick to what you need to say. For example, if you need to warn someone that her job is in jeopardy unless her performance improves, it's really important that you say those actual words and not soften them in the moment—but that's also the hardest part to say. Practicing out loud can get you more comfortable with the language and reduce the chances that you'll dilute the message when you do it for real.

1. You have concerns about someone's work

It can be painful to tell someone his work isn't good enough, but it's essential that you be willing to have that conversation—and not put it off. Allowing someone to continue producing mediocre or worse work will impact your team's results, as well as the person's professional reputation, evaluations, and potentially compensation and even his ability to stay in the job.

What to say depends on whether your concerns are project-specific or of a broader nature.

If your feedback is specific to one particular project, it's an easier conversation. You can just be straightforward about what needs to be done differently. And you can even treat it as a communication issue more than a work quality issue—since, if it's not part of a broader pattern, that's likely the case. For example:

- *"I realize that I didn't fully communicate what was in my head on this project. Because this will be seen by a wide audience, it needs to be more polished and provide more background. That means . . ."*

If the problem is broader than that, then what you really need to give feedback on is the *pattern,* not individual projects. Often when there's a pattern of problems with someone's work, managers keep addressing the individual instances and assume that the employee will connect the dots, but they never explicitly say "Hey, this is a pattern." And as a result, sometimes people don't realize that it's a pattern, and a serious problem.

The basic formula for pattern feedback is this: "I've noticed this pattern in your work, and here's what I need instead." For example:

- *"We've talked a few times recently about how I need you to do a better job of following through on assignments and making sure that nothing slips through the cracks, but it's still happening. It's become a pattern, and I'm concerned because really tight follow-through is crucial for success in this job. Can we talk about what you think has been happening and what you can do differently going forward?"*

If you don't see the improvement you need after that, then in most cases you'd move to addressing the issue as a serious performance problem (and possibly a fit-for-the-role issue). But often just naming the pattern can help the person get back on track or figure out what help he might need to do that.

2. Asking someone to stop socializing at work so much

Some socializing in an office is a good thing; employees who get along well are more likely to work together effectively. And most people need small breaks during the day, so some amount of chatting is normal.

Most important, if someone is a good employee who gets good results in her work, micromanaging how she spends her time can be demoralizing and counterproductive. In general, you want to err on the side of trusting people to manage their own time as long as the work is getting done, and done well.

But if you manage someone whose chattiness is a problem—either because it's hindering her own productivity or because it's distracting other people—at that point you have to say something.

- If you think the socializing is impacting the employee's own productivity: Talk about your productivity concerns (what things aren't getting done as quickly as you'd like) and then say, *"I've noticed that you spend a fair amount of time chatting with coworkers, and it's pulling your focus away from work. That might be part of the problem. Can you cut back on that and see if it helps?"*

- If the socializing is distracting others: *"I've noticed that you're spending a fair amount of time chatting with Isabelle during the day. I know that you're good at managing your workload and I don't have concerns about your productivity, but that much chitchat in the office can be distracting to other people. Can I ask you to cut back on it for that reason?"*

3. Employee is spending too much time on social media during the workday

If every time you pass your employee's desk, you notice that he's scrolling through Facebook or Twitter, the first question is what kind of results he's getting in his work. If his work is stellar, err on the side of assuming that he can manage his own time (since clearly he must be doing that effectively). But if that's not the case, it's reasonable to say something, especially if you suspect a connection between the person's focus and his productivity. For example:

- *"I don't mind if you take the occasional break to check the Internet or your phone, but what I'm seeing is more than occasional. I'd like you to rein it in, especially when there are outstanding projects or emails that people are waiting to hear back on."*

- *"I've noticed you're spending a lot of time on the Internet, and I want to be transparent with you that it's made me wonder about how you're managing your time. Can we talk through how you're allocating your time and setting your priorities?"*

4. Staff member is blowing deadlines

When you and a staff member agree on a deadline and then that deadline is missed, it's important to follow up and find out what happened. If you don't do that, you're setting yourself up for missed deadlines in the future, since your staff member may conclude that letting deadlines slip is no big deal.

But this doesn't have to be a big, scary, bring-out-the-tissues conversation. In most cases, just asking "What happened?" is enough to signal that you're paying attention and will create accountability. It can be this simple:

- *"We had set last night as the deadline for getting this to me. What happened there?"*

In fact, "What happened?" is an incredibly useful question for any situation where you need to create accountability and make it clear that whatever happened wasn't okay and shouldn't happen again. It also opens the door for your staff member to tell you something relevant that you didn't know (like "Our power was out and I couldn't get online to email it to you" or "I was in the hospital").

If the issue is a chronic one and your staff member is blowing deadlines repeatedly, change the formulation to "What's going on?" or "What's been happening?" For example:

• *"You've been missing deadlines recently, like the video blog yesterday and the grant report last month. What's been happening?"*

Again, this gives the person the opportunity to tell you things you might not know, like that someone else is getting in the way of her finishing her work or even that deadlines haven't been as clear as you thought they were. But if nothing like that emerges, then you should do the following:

1. **Explain the impact of the missed deadlines.** For example: *"When you get me work later than we agreed, it has a domino effect on me and others. I end up having to stay late to review it or having to push others later in the process to rush their pieces of it, or we look bad to buyers when we don't meet our timeline commitments. When we agree on a deadline, I'm planning based on that agreement, so it's really important to stick to that timeline or to give me early warning—before any deadline is missed—if you're concerned about whether you'll be able to meet it."*

2. **Ask what system your staff member is using to track deadlines and her work overall.** Does she have a system, or is she relying on memory? Is she working on things far enough in advance or is she waiting until the last minute and then running out of time? Depending on what you find out, she might need some coaching on different systems or work habits that would solve the problem.

3. **Be clear about your expectations going forward.** It's okay to be pretty directive here, since a pattern of missed deadlines is serious. For example: *"Okay, going forward, we're in agreement that you'll start working on projects earlier so that you have a buffer if it turns out you need more time. You'll try the new calendaring system we discussed, and you'll come talk to me well in advance if you have any worries about your ability to meet a deadline. Does that sound right to you?"*

5. Employee says his workload is too heavy but you don't think it is

If you have an employee who says that his workload is too much and your gut tells you that it should be manageable, it's worth doing more digging before coming to any conclusions. Don't be afraid to ask questions to get a better understanding of the details of the workload and how long things take and why. Think, too, about what you've seen high performers in similar roles do, since that's a good source of data about what you can reasonably expect.

But if you determine that the person in the job really should be able to handle the workload, a good formula for talking about it is "I hear you, but what I need in the role is . . ." For example:

- *"I hear you that it's a lot of work and it can be a challenge to keep everything moving, but I do need this role to juggle a high volume of work. My sense is that we could be turning around X much more quickly and hitting higher numbers on Y."*

6. Staff member gets defensive when you correct her work

Defensiveness is one of the most difficult responses to deal with when giving a staff member feedback, because it can prevent the person from really hearing and processing what you're saying. And, human nature being what it is, it can make you less inclined to give feedback in the future, because encountering defensiveness can make the experience so unpleasant.

The key to responding to defensiveness is to name it and identify it as a problem in and of itself. For example:

- *"I've noticed that when we talk about things you could do differently, you often push back and say there's no reason to change anything. At times it can come across as defensive or even argumentative."*

Then stop and listen to how your staff member responds. She might be surprised that she's coming across that way, or might argue that her responses have been justified. If she continues to be defensive, you could explain further:

- *"When you respond that way, it makes it hard for me to talk to you about things I'd like you to try doing differently. I need to be able to bring you concerns or suggestions and have you really hear me. If you have a different perspective, I welcome hearing it, but ultimately I need you to hear me, too, and if you're automatically pushing back, it makes that difficult."*

- *"When I give you input about things you could do differently in your work, I'm not being adversarial. It's how*

*people learn and get better at what they do. We're partners
in this work, and part of my role is to help you get stronger
at what you do. Feedback isn't a message that you're failing!
It's about how to grow in your job. Do you think you can
try seeing it from that perspective in the future?"*

In this conversation, pay particular attention to your tone.
Because the person is already feeling defensive, you don't
want your tone to sound as if you're criticizing her for an additional thing. Instead, your tone should convey, "I think
you do good work and I want to help you do even better."

7. Telling someone to stop complaining about a coworker

If an employee won't stop complaining about a colleague,
you need to be able to say "Enough" without inadvertently
shutting down future input that might be important for you
to hear.

To do that, express that (a) you've heard the person out,
(b) you've considered his perspective, and (c) continuing to
bring up the topic isn't constructive and is becoming a distraction. (And if circumstances allow you to explain why you
don't agree with your employee's opinion, ideally you should
do that, too.)

Here's what this conversation might sound like:

- *"I've heard what you've said, and I appreciate your sharing
your perspective with me. I've looked into what you've told
me, and my take is different from yours because _____. I
hear you that you disagree, but it's becoming a distraction
to keep discussing it. At this point, we need to move forward. I welcome your feedback about what you need in*

your work, but I need it to be about you and not about Julian. Can you do that going forward?"

Alternately, if you agree with the person's take and you're working on addressing it behind the scenes, you might say something like this:

- *"I appreciate your sharing this with me, and I can understand your frustration. I'm going to be handling this, but I want you to know that I'm going to deal with it privately, so you may not see immediate evidence of that."* (Or, *"I'm addressing it in the way I think will be most effective."*) *"From here on, I want to know if something changes, but otherwise please trust that I'm on this."*

8. Employee does good work but has terrible relationships with coworkers

When someone does good work but can't seem to get along with any of his coworkers, some managers hesitate to intervene. They often worry that interpersonal skills aren't as legitimate an area for coaching and direction as, say, coding or presentation skills. But maintaining decent relationships with coworkers—at least being pleasant and civil to them—is as much a part of most people's job as anything else is. It's your job to explain that and hold the person accountable for it:

- *"Part of your job is maintaining good relationships with other people on our team. When people don't want to talk to you, they go around you, which makes our work less efficient. More broadly, when you're snapping at people or otherwise being grumpy with them, it makes for an unpleasant environment for everyone around you. To succeed in this role, it's*

*not enough just to write great code. You also need to main-
tain good relationships with colleagues, because we're not a
one-person shop. That includes not rolling your eyes at people, not snapping at them, and generally putting some effort
into making your interactions with other people pleasant."*

9. Two employees aren't getting along

When two employees aren't getting along, the first question
to ask yourself is: Is this conflict affecting their work or pos-
ing a problem for other employees? If two people simply
don't like each other, that's fine—they're not required to. But
they can't act in ways that create an uncomfortable environment for other people, and they do need to deal with each
other pleasantly and professionally. If that's not happening,
you need to intervene.

First, it's worth getting a better understanding of what the
conflict is about, because it might be rooted in genuine work
issues. If one person is frustrated because the other keeps
missing deadlines that hold up her work or is rude to clients,
you'll need to deal with that root cause as well.

From there, though, talk with each person individually
and say something like this:

• *"I understand that you've had some conflict with Morgan.
I don't need to know the whole story, unless there's a work
concern that you want to share with me, but I do need both
of you to behave pleasantly and professionally to all of your
coworkers, including each other. I'm making the same
thing clear to Morgan. You don't have to like each other,
but you do need to treat each other civilly. That's just a
basic part of the job for anyone working here. Can you do
that going forward?"*

In some cases, it will be just one person who has been treating the other poorly. In that case, it's worth saying to the target of the mistreatment:

- *"I've told Fernando that he's required to treat you politely and respectfully. If that continues not to happen, I need you to let me know so that I can intervene further."*

10. Staff member is too long-winded

If you have an employee who rambles and gives you long, drawn-out answers when you need something more concise, this is something that you can give feedback on! In fact, not just *can*, but *should*—because the habit is probably holding the person back professionally.

Try saying something like this:

- *"Can I give you some feedback? When I ask you questions, you're very thorough in your answers. That's great in some situations, and I love that you know your stuff so well, but more often than not, I don't need so much information. I trust that you're handling the details competently, and generally I'm just looking for the quick summary on whatever I ask about—the key headlines. I'll let you know if I need more, but often I don't."*

You might give a specific example or two as well:

- *"To give you an example of what I mean, when I asked you earlier today where we were with the billboard design, I just needed to know that it's on track to be finalized tomorrow, not the whole context about the issues with the font selection. It's important that that context be handled well, of course, but I trust you to take care of it and just bring me in if you need my input on something specific."*

From there, as you move forward, it might help to give the staff member clear time cues to help her remember to keep it brief. For example, you might say things like:

- *"Could you give me a quick one-minute overview of X?"*

- *"We have twenty minutes scheduled, and I'm hoping we can cover X, Y, and Z in that time."*

11. Employee's stress impacts the whole team

If someone vents about stress constantly or just doesn't control it well, that can end up stressing out everyone around him. If this is happening on your team, start by talking with the person one-on-one and asking what's going on:

- *"You seem pretty stressed lately. What's going on?"*

This might lead to a conversation where you can provide concrete help with things like prioritizing the person's workload, adjusting deadlines, or suggesting shortcuts or more efficient ways to approach a project. But if the person is stressed out by things that are just normal parts of the job—issues where there aren't really solutions other than "just roll with it"—then you may need to explain that, name the fact that his stress is affecting other people, and ask about other ways it might be managed:

- *"I hear you that it can be stressful to have to get input from so many people and to make last-minute changes sometimes. It's really the nature of the role, though; those things are pretty unavoidable in this type of work. When you complain frequently to coworkers about it and start most meetings by talking about how frazzled you are, it can raise the stress level for everyone. Do you think you can find other ways to manage your stress so that it doesn't spread to your coworkers as well?"*

Depending on how the conversation goes, you might add:

- *"I want to be clear that I'm not asking you never to feel stressed. I know this work can be stressful! Rather, this is about being aware of how your handling of stress might be affecting colleagues. You can of course come and talk to me when you're feeling overwhelmed; I want to be a resource for you when that's happening. It's adding to other people's stress levels that I want to avoid."*

12. Employee made a serious mistake

Assuming that you employ humans, at some point one of them is going to make a pretty significant mistake. When that happens, your role is to (a) ensure that your employee understands the seriousness of the mistake, (b) find out how it happened so that you can ensure that there are plans in place to prevent something similar in the future, and (c) if it's part of a pattern, address that pattern.

What you *don't* need to do is berate or punish the person who made the mistake. Of course, if the person seems unconcerned, figure out why—but conscientious employees are likely already berating themselves, and you don't need to add to that.

Here's how the conversation might go:

- First, ask for your employee's perspective so that you get a sense of how she sees the situation and how seriously she's taking the problem: *"Can we talk about what happened at the conference? I know there was a lot of confusion over who was speaking where, and some VIPs were locked out of sessions they were supposed to be attending. What happened?"*

- If you don't get a sense that the person recognizes how serious the mistake is, address that; otherwise, skip this step: *"This is a pretty serious mistake. It reflects badly on us to important people who were doing us a favor by attending, and makes us look like we don't have our act together."*

- Ask how the person will avoid similar mistakes in the future: *"What are your thoughts about what you could have done differently, and what you'll do differently in the future?"*

It generally doesn't make sense to fire someone for a single mistake if the person's work is otherwise good, even if the mistake is a serious one, especially since most competent people will be extremely careful never to make that mistake again. But if the mistake is part of a larger pattern, like sloppiness or poor judgment, that's a different story. In that case, at a minimum you'll need to address the situation more broadly as well (see conversation 1 in this chapter), and you should probably be thinking about whether the person is the right match for the job.

13. You asked someone to stay late or work over the weekend to fix a problem that you caused

Sometimes, as a manager, you will have to ask people to stay late or work over the weekend to finish up something time-sensitive. Your employees, if they're reasonable people, understand this. But an occasional "necessary fact of life" can quickly turn into a "frustrating and demoralizing imposition" when the request could have been avoided with better planning on your part.

But that doesn't mean it'll never happen—it's a reality of managing, and you're not infallible. When it does happen, though, it's important that you acknowledge what happened (definitely don't try to pretend the situation is anything other than it really is or you will destroy your credibility), apologize, and express sincere appreciation for your employees' extra trouble. (And of course, work hard to avoid its happening with any frequency.)

Try saying something like this:

- *"I misunderstood our deadline for this project and thought we had until Monday to finish it. It turns out we don't, and we actually need to send it to the printer tomorrow in order to make our mail deadline. This is one hundred percent on me, but can I ask you to help me get it into workable shape before tomorrow morning? I know that's going to mess up your evening, and I'm so sorry to ask it. I wouldn't make the request if it weren't crucial."*

Contrast the above with the responsibility-avoiding version, which sounds like this: "We need to get this to the printer tomorrow, so I need you to finish writing it tonight."

You can see how that's much more likely to leave employees feeling resentful and wondering why they have to clean up a mistake that you're not even acknowledging you made.

14. An employee cries when you give her feedback

If you manage enough people for long enough, at some point someone is going to cry in your office—most likely when you're talking about something that went wrong with her work.

As awkward as you might feel when this happens, the person crying almost certainly feels even more awkward about it. Because of that, if the person is just a little tearful, the kindest course is often simply to continue the conversation rather than draw attention to the crying. But if that's not practical, or you worry it would come across as callous, try saying something like:

• *"I can see you're upset. Would you like me to give you a few minutes?"*

If the crying happens frequently, you might say:

• *"I can see that these conversations are hard for you. Is there anything I can do differently to make them easier on you?"*

You might find out that the person would appreciate a short heads-up about the issues in an email before you meet, or maybe she just needs a minute to compose herself, or perhaps there's some other solution that would help.

In some cases, the crying itself might be causing problems. If, for example, it's making people afraid to talk to the person, or if it's so out of place in your office culture that it's harming the person's reputation, then that's worth addressing on its own. In that case, you can be empathetic while also being candid about the impact it's having. For example:

- *"I know tearing up can be an involuntary reaction. I'm concerned, though, that it's happening often enough that people are becoming reluctant to tell you when something has gone wrong. I know there may not be an easy fix, but I want to make you aware of the impact I'm seeing it have."*

Am I saying "I'm sorry" to employees too often?

A reader writes:
I'm a new manager at a company where I've worked for years. In trying to adjust to the role, I'm realizing that I'm the sort of person who says "sorry" a lot. I'm not always doing it to take the blame on myself; I'm often doing it because I think it shows empathy and sometimes makes a situation less confrontational. Do you think this is hurting my effectiveness? I think I can apologize in ways that are still appropriately firm (e.g., "I'm sorry, I know this is piling on to an already busy week, but I need you to add X to your plate and get it done by Friday"), but am I actually undermining myself by doing this?

I think it depends on how often you're saying it.

In the example you gave, where you're adding something on to an already full plate, it makes sense to acknowledge that. It would be a bad thing if you *didn't* acknowledge it.

On the other hand, if you're apologizing every time you delegate work to someone, that's going to quickly become weird, because it will start to sound like you feel sheepish about delegating, which will make your employees feel awkward and wonder why you're not more matter-of-fact about exercising normal authority.

So it's a matter of balance. The expression isn't inherently problematic, but if you find yourself saying "I'm sorry" constantly, then yeah, I'd rein it in.

And if you're using it to show empathy, keep in mind that you have a bunch of other tools at your disposal to do that. Thanking people, in a genuine way, for taking on extra work is one way. Making real efforts to help people manage a high workload is one more. Urging people to take a day or afternoon off when their workload allows it is still another. These things have a much bigger impact than just acknowledging "Yeah, this sucks, and I wish it didn't," so make sure you're doing them, too.

But again: "I'm sorry" is fine, in moderation. The overall picture is what you want to pay attention to.

15. You heard that one of your employees is interviewing for a new job

If you hear that one of your staff members is job-searching, it's in your best interests to stay calm and show that you understand it's not personal. Whatever you do, don't guilt-trip the person or act angry or betrayed, or you will push the person out the door faster. People leaving jobs is a normal part of business; it's not a personal betrayal! Plus, if your other employees hear that you reacted badly to their coworker's job search, they're likely to make damn sure to keep their own job searches under wraps when the time comes, which means that you'll be forfeiting any possibility of generous notice periods from most or all of your staff.

If the employee is someone you value and don't want to lose, say something like this:

- *"I know this is awkward, but I overheard you talking about interviewing for a new job. You don't need to confirm that if you don't want to, but I want to let you know that I value your work very highly and hope that you'll stay with us for a long time. If you* are *thinking about leaving, I'd really appreciate the chance to see if we can find a way to keep you happy here before you make any decisions."*

In addition, do some thinking on your own about what might be driving the person to job-search. Money? Promotion potential? Frustrations with the job or with coworkers? There might be an obvious problem that you need to address before you can credibly ask the person to consider staying.

And of course, if this isn't someone you'd be devastated to lose, there's not really anything here that you need to speak up about. In that case, it's fine to just mentally file away the information and let the situation play out on its own.

16. Telling an employee to dress more professionally

Telling an employee to dress more professionally can be tough, because it feels like personal criticism (as opposed to work-related feedback, which you're probably—hopefully— more used to giving).

To make it feel less personal, it can help to think about it like this: The way the employee dresses is fine for her outside life; it's just not appropriate for this particular office or this particular job. So it's not about judging her personal style; it's just about ensuring that her choices are appropriate in this context.

It helps, too, to go into the conversation thinking, "I want to help this person be noticed for her work rather than her clothes." That mindset is likely to help you make it clear that you're on her side, which will make the conversation easier on both of you.

From there, frame it like any other conversation where you're asking an employee to change something about her work. Here are some ways to say it:

- *"We have a relatively conservative dress code here, and it's important that you look put together. When you wear wrinkled or stained clothes, or sneakers instead of business-style shoes, it doesn't look pulled together enough for your role."*

- *"You always look very fashionable, but some of your clothes are a bit too revealing for the office. Higher necklines and*

skirts that hit closer to the knee work better in our environ-
ment and will help you be seen as the talented professional
you are."

- *"I appreciate how professional you always are, but in our*
  environment, we can't wear skirts quite that short. Stick
  with knee-length or just above the knee and you'll be fine."

- For a younger employee who might still be figuring out
  professional dress, you might offer advice from your own
  experience: *"I know that when you're just starting out, it*
  can be tricky to figure out what is and isn't appropriate for
  the office, especially on a junior salary. I went through that
  myself a few years ago, and here's what I found worked
  pretty well . . ."

Of course, it doesn't always have to be a Big Conversation.
If the problem isn't a chronic one, often it can simply be addressed with a quick, "Hey, our dress code actually says no
tennis shoes. Can you remember that going forward?"

17. Addressing body odor

This is a situation even the most experienced managers dread:
telling an employee that he smells.

Most of us have very little practice delivering this kind of
awkward and highly personal message, but you do need to do
it, because it's likely affecting the way your staff member is
perceived (and even the way your company is perceived if the
person deals with clients or visitors to your office), and it's
probably affecting his coworkers as well.

Meet with the employee privately, preferably at the end of
the day (so that he doesn't have to feel self-conscious sitting

at work for hours afterward), and be honest, direct, and as kind as possible. Say something like this:

• *"I want to discuss something that's awkward, and I hope I don't offend you. I've noticed you've had a noticeable odor lately. It might mean a need to wash clothes more frequently or shower more often, or it could be a medical problem. This is the kind of thing that people often don't realize about themselves, so I wanted to bring it to your attention and ask you to see what you can do about it."*

Note that this language doesn't mention complaints from coworkers, even if you'd heard some; it's keeping it focused on what *you* have noticed. That's because you don't want to make your employee feel even more awkward by indicating that multiple people have been talking about this.

18. Employee seems chronically unhappy at work

If you have an employee who seems chronically unhappy at work, it's worth having a conversation to see what's going on. (Note, though, that "chronically" is key—you don't want to swoop in demanding answers from someone who's just having a bad week.) The idea here is to find out if there are problems that you might be able to help solve, expectations about the work that are out of sync with reality, or anything else that might benefit from open conversation about what's going on.

The best opener for this kind of conversation is a simple one. Just ask this:

• *"How are things going for you at work lately?"*

That might be all you need to ask to get the employee talking! Some people will open up in response to a simple invitation like this. Others, of course, won't, in which case you could move to:

- *"I might be misinterpreting, but you've seemed pretty down lately. I wondered if there's anything going on workwise that's bothering you. If there is, I'd really like to try to talk through it with you and see if it's something that we can fix."*

If things have gotten to the point where the person's unhappiness is getting in the way of her doing her job (or where she's becoming disruptive to others), that's a different conversation. You still might start with the above, but there may come a point where the conversation you need to have is this one:

- *"I know you've had some serious frustrations with your work recently. We've talked about your concerns with tight deadlines and having to incorporate input from Rupert that you don't always agree with, and while I hear what you're saying, I also want to be up-front with you about the fact that those things aren't going to change. They're really inherent parts of the job. I don't want us to have to constantly battle over them—that's not good for you and, frankly, it's not great for me either. Would it make sense for you to figure out if there's a way for you to be reasonably happy in the job, knowing that the things that have frustrated you aren't going to change? If the job just isn't what you want, I would understand that and would work with you on a transition if that's what makes the most sense for you. And to be clear, I'm not pushing you out—I think you do great work and want to keep you around—but I also can't keep fighting these same battles, and I doubt you want to either."*

19. Asking an employee to stop working from home so frequently

Letting employees work from home when their jobs allow it is the kind of flexibility that tends to keep people happy with their work. But there are times when you might need to ask someone to work from home less often—like when they're missing important ad hoc conversations that would benefit their work, when they're not sufficiently accessible to co-workers, or when their colleagues are being forced to pick up their work in the office.

In doing this, be explicit about what you want ("Work from home less" isn't nearly as clear as "I'd like you to limit your work-from-home days to twice a month"), and explain your reasoning so that it doesn't feel arbitrary or punitive:

- *"I want to talk with you about how often you're working from home. I'm glad to give you the flexibility when the work allows for it, and I know how valuable it is to be able to focus without distractions. But I also think there's real value in being here in the office, because the nature of our jobs means we have a lot of ad hoc conversations that our work really benefits from—like the spontaneous problem-solving we did as a group last week about challenges finding event space. Given that, I'd like your default to be working from home no more than twice a month. I know we haven't clarified this earlier, so you haven't done anything wrong by doing it more often—this is just about how to handle it going forward."*

20. Addressing sexist or racist comments

If you hear an employee make a sexist, racist, or otherwise bigoted comment, you *have* to address it because you have both a legal and a moral obligation to ensure that your other employees aren't subjected to bigoted comments or behavior.

If there are other people around when you hear the comment, you should ideally address it right on the spot— because otherwise you risk having people think that you're fine with whatever was said, which can make for a really uncomfortable environment for your other employees.

Ways to address it on the spot include:

- *"I'm sure you didn't mean it this way, but that term is actually considered problematic because of _____."*

- *"Whoa, we value customers and employees of all races and religions here. I hope you didn't really mean that."*

- *"Hey, that kind of comment is not okay here."*

If you're not able to address it in the moment, follow up as soon as you can. At that point, you might say:

- *"I heard you say something earlier that concerned me. I'm sure you didn't mean it this way, but saying _____ comes across as if you mean _____."*

- *"You made a comment earlier that didn't sit right with me, and I wanted to ask you about it. You said _____, which I took to mean _____. Did I understand you correctly?"*

- *"I want to be really clear that that kind of comment isn't okay here. I need you to be respectful to people regardless of their sex/race/religion. Can you do that going forward?"*

My older employee keeps talking about my age

A reader writes:
I recently started a brand-new position. They hired me as the department manager and also hired a project coordinator, who reports to me. We have just completed our first week together.

It has become quickly obvious that my direct report has a major issue with my age (I would guess I am twenty years younger than she is). She keeps making comments like "Gosh, it's crazy to have a supervisor who is the same age as my daughter" or "This structure will be an adjustment for me, I am used to being in the driver's seat. Good for you for advancing in your career so quickly."

I've tried to use subtle humor tactics to deflect these remarks and pivot from her age hang-ups, but they continue to sneak in. How should I proceed? It doesn't help that we are both new and she obviously feels like we are on equal footing. For the record, I am not that young (thirty-seven) nor do I look youthful (despite all those expensive face creams).

When subtle humor works in these situations, it can be a great thing; it can let the other person save face and let you both avoid an awkward conversation. But think of it as a one-shot deal; if the message doesn't seem to land, then you need to move on to a more direct conversation. Continuing to just hint or pivot is too passive an approach for a manager/employee relationship.

So it's time to switch over to being very direct. The next time she makes a comment about your age, stop the conversation and address it right in the moment: "Jane, you've mentioned our relative ages several times. I'm assuming it won't be an issue for you." And then just stop and see what she says. She may squirm, she may be embarrassed, or she may dig in her heels and make another comment about how it's just unusual for her. If she does the latter, then you should say, "It doesn't strike me as odd, and I'd rather we not get sidetracked by it."

Hopefully this will be enough to convey to her that the comments need to stop. But if not and she continues to make this kind of remark, watch to see how frequent they are as she gets settled in, and also how aggressive they are. If it's just a couple more comments and they're not particularly egregious, I'd let it go—there's actually power in not being rattled by it, and in not feeling you have to address every little challenge to your authority. But if it's frequent or aggressive, then yeah, you do need to stamp it out with something like, "Our ages really aren't relevant here. Is there a reason you keep mentioning them?"

My bigger worry, though, would be whether these are just naïve and clumsy comments, or whether they indicate a deeper problem with reporting to someone younger. If they're just annoying comments, you can probably afford to move past them pretty quickly. But if

she resents having you as her manager or doesn't respect your ability to do your job, that's an issue you'll
need to nip in the bud by addressing it just as you would
any other performance issue. For example: "I've noticed
you seem reluctant to take on assignments I give you.
What's going on?" Or, "We agreed that you'd do X, but
you did Y. What happened?" . . . escalating to, if it continues, "In this role, I need you to do XYZ. Can you do
that going forward?"

Meanwhile, though, the best thing that you can do is
treat her as though you haven't even noticed your age
difference. Don't let yourself feel awkward about it; remember that you were hired for a reason, and operate
with the confidence of your position.

21. Employee is habitually late

If an employee is regularly late to work, the first question to
ask is whether it truly affects her work or her coworkers.
There are lots of jobs where a bit of lateness truly won't
impact an employee's effectiveness, and if that's the case,
you should take that into account. But if the lateness does
affect the person's work, or other people, then you need to
step in.

If it's the first conversation you've had about the lateness,
say this:

- *"I've noticed that you've been coming in late recently. I
need you to be here reliably by nine each morning because
otherwise people end up calling Paige when they can't reach
you. Can you make sure you're here on time from now on?"*

If the problem continues after that:

- *"We've talked before about the need for you to be here no later than nine, but you're continuing to arrive late, which leaves us short-staffed. What's going on?"*

Depending on the answer, you might then say:

- *"I hear you that traffic can be unpredictable, and I wish I could give you more flexibility. The job really does require being here by nine, though, which may mean that you need to leave earlier in the mornings, even if that means sometimes you'll get here earlier than you need to. Is that something you can find a way to do going forward?"*

- *"I do need you to arrive on time every day. It's not a requirement for every job, but for this one, phones start ringing right at nine and we need you here to answer them. Knowing that we can't be flexible on that, is there a way for you to make this job and this schedule work?"*

- *"I hear you that you're in a tough spot with childcare, and I wish I could give you more flexibility. The job really does require being here by nine, though. I can give you a few weeks to try to firm up your childcare arrangements, but after that I really do need to hold you to that start time."*

- When you can offer a schedule change: *"I hear you that you're in a tough spot with childcare. Would it make sense to look at officially changing your start time so that you're coming in a little later and leaving a little later at the end of the day?"*

22. Employee is "out sick" but posting photos from the beach on social media

First things first: Are you absolutely sure the employee isn't actually home sick? People sometimes post vacation or other photos after the fact, so simply seeing them show up on a sick day isn't evidence that the person isn't actually at home sick. You don't want to be the boss who comes down on someone for lying when in fact the person was in bed nursing strep throat.

But if you do know for sure—for example, if the employee is tagging herself as being in Ocean City rather than at home in Virginia, or is writing about a trip in the present tense—then you might choose to say something, if for no other reason than that unplanned, last-minute sick days tend to be more disruptive than scheduled vacation days. (Plus, obviously, the lying is a problem.)

There are a couple of ways to address this:

- The low-key "I know what you did on your sick day" method: *"Did you intend to charge yesterday to sick leave or vacation leave? I saw you mention on Facebook that you were in Ocean City."*

- The more direct approach: *"I saw your posts on Facebook about being in Ocean City. I had thought you were taking a sick day yesterday. Did we cross wires?"*

Note that neither of these begins with an accusation. That's because if it does turn out that you're wrong, having started with an accusation will poison the relationship. Just seek information first. If it does turn out that you were right, then you can say something like this:

- *"I support you in getting the time off you need, but sick leave is different from vacation leave because it's unplanned, which means it can be more of a disruption of our work. Going forward, if you need a last-minute day off, come talk to me and we'll see what we can work out—but I'd like you to reserve sick leave for when you're sick. That's what it's for."*

All that said . . . even good employees play hooky occasionally. If the person is otherwise an excellent employee and this is a one-time event that didn't impact anyone's work, the smartest move might be to let it go and not bother with the conversation.

Should you connect with employees on social media?

By all means, go ahead and connect with employees on LinkedIn—because it's a professional networking site. But when it comes to Facebook and other more social sites, connecting with people you manage can cause real problems. You might see things about their politics, health, or personal life that they might prefer you not know. Or, as in conversation 22, you might see things that will make you uneasy, like that someone was out clubbing all night before she called in sick. It's a lot cleaner to just avoid all those potential complications and have an across-the-board policy of not friending people you manage.

23. Employee is missing too much work

The first thing to do when an employee is missing a lot of work is to ask, "What's going on?" You want to start there because you might learn that the employee is dealing with serious health issues, or is caring for an ill family member, or has other highly sympathetic reasons for missing work. That doesn't always mean that you'll be able to accommodate a high number of absences, but it should at least inform the way you proceed and how you talk with the person.

From there . . .

- If the person has a running litany of excuses: *"I hear you that you've had a run of bad luck, but I need to be able to count on you to be here reliably. Certainly life will intervene from time to time, but the frequency of your absences has been too high. Going forward, I need you here every day unless we've approved the time off in advance or there's a very unusual circumstance, which I wouldn't expect to happen more than a few times a year. Can you commit to doing that?"*

- If the reason is more sympathetic but you must also convey that you need more reliable attendance: *"I know you're having a tough time right now, and I'm so sorry you're dealing with that. We're at the point where the number of times you're out is starting to impact your work and other people's, so I want to talk about possible solutions."* (Depending on the circumstances and what's feasible for you and the employee, here you might suggest moving temporarily to a part-time schedule so that the person's workload better fits her availability, taking a short-term medical leave of absence, or other accommodations that might get you both closer to what you need.)

24. Employee is relying too much on your help

If you have an employee who defaults to bringing you problems to solve rather than trying to resolve them on her own first, explain that you'd like her to operate in a different way:

- *"I'm happy to be a resource when you're stuck, but I'd like to see you trying to problem-solve on your own first. I think you'll come to a lot of these answers if you trust your instincts and spend some time thinking problems through on your own. You can also check the department manual, which has some of these answers in it. If you're still stuck after that, come to me—but let's make it your default that you'll try to find the answers yourself first."*

After that, if the employee brings you issues that you think she should have been able to solve on her own, say something like:

- *"What have you considered so far?"*

- *"This is the sort of question where I'd love for you to devise a solution for yourself. What have you tried so far?"*

- *"What do you think would make sense here?"*

25. Staff member is afraid to take on new things

When an employee is resistant to taking on new projects or responsibilities, sometimes it's because the person is already stretched thin (which is legitimate, and then you should dig in and help prioritize). But if your sense is that the resistance comes from fear of taking on something unfamiliar, that's worth addressing head-on.

Acknowledge that it's a new type of work, explain why you think the person will be good at it, and offer yourself (or another appropriate colleague) as a resource. For example:

- *"I hear you that this is new and unfamiliar. I think you'll be great at it because you've shown such skill with X and Y, and I've seen you master new types of work pretty quickly in the past. But we're not going to just throw you to the wolves. We'll figure out the beginning stages together, and I'll help support you as you get acclimated to it. And Persephone has done this type of work before and will be a great person to provide advice."*

If you've noticed that the resistance is part of a pattern, you might say something like this:

- *"I've noticed you tend to be hesitant to take on new types of work. But you're actually very good at learning new things once you start to feel comfortable. I want to see you continue to grow and stretch in this role, and I know from watching you in the past that you're more than capable of delivering on this."*

If you continue to encounter resistance and you need to convey that the person truly does need to take on the new project or responsibility, say this:

- *"I hear what you're saying. I do need you to take this on, but we can revisit it in a month and make sure it's going well."*

Of course, be sure that you're reading the person's resistance correctly! You don't want to inadvertently mistake a well-founded concern about an overwhelming workload or a lack of training for a confidence issue.

26. Employee's expectations for the job are unrealistic

If you have an employee who seems to expect the job to be something different from what it actually is, the best thing that you can do is to confront the issue head-on. In doing this, be very straightforward about what the reality of the job is, so that you can figure out whether the person actually wants the job she's in or not.

For example, if you have a junior-level employee who thinks she should be doing more senior-level work than what you want to give her, you might say something like this:

- *"It sounds like you're hoping to do more strategy work and interviews with reporters. I want to be up-front with you that this job is really about writing blog posts and managing our social media. You'll be able to sit in on strategy meetings sometimes, but this isn't a spokesperson role where you'd be doing interviews. I hope that, knowing this, you'll still be*

enthusiastic about the job—but if you're not, I of course un-
derstand. Do you want to take some time to think about it?"

If the person is extremely talented, add some extra encour-
agement by saying something like:

• *"I do think you're extremely talented, and the experience*
you're getting here is going to give you a good foundation to
move in that direction in the future. And we can make a
point of investing in developing your skills to help with
that. But I want to be very up-front with you about what
the role is and isn't right now."

27. Telling an employee to stop going over your head

If an employee keeps going over your head to your own boss,
when he should be coming to you instead, it can be hard to
know how to address it without sounding like you're trying to
hide things from your boss. But the chain of command exists
for a reason, and it's okay to tell people that they need to use it.
    You can say it like this:

• *"I've noticed that you've been taking issues like X and Y to*
Maria. Part of my job is to handle those issues so that
Maria doesn't have to—and frankly, I need to be in the
loop earlier because I sometimes have info that Maria
doesn't have. Going forward, please come talk to me about
those things. If we're not able to resolve something ourselves,
I may loop her in—but I need you to start with me."

Depending on how your boss has been handling it when
your employee goes to her, you might also ask her to direct

the person back to you. If you don't get the sense that your boss understands why it's important for her to do that, you can try saying something like this:

- *"People should definitely be able to talk with you if they've been unable to resolve something with me that's important enough to escalate, but I'd like them to talk with me first so that I'm in the loop and can attempt to address the issue. Otherwise I worry that it undermines my ability to manage them. If Dante comes to you in the future, would you try redirecting him back to me by asking if he's talked with me about the issue and, if he hasn't, telling him to do that first?"*

28. Setting boundaries with an employee who treats you like a BFF

As a manager, you can be *friendly* with the people who work for you, but you can't be *friends*. You're on an inherently unequal footing, and you need to be able to honestly evaluate people's work, give tough feedback, and even potentially let someone go at some point. Plus, appearances matter, and if people see that you're personal friends with someone on your team, they're likely to assume you're playing favorites, no matter how hard you try to be impartial.

So if you have someone on your team who's making it hard to maintain that boundary—confiding in you about personal matters, inviting you to one-on-one social occasions, or otherwise treating you more like a BFF than a boss—you have to set a firmer boundary. Sometimes you can do this through subtle cues—declining invitations, wrapping up too-personal conversations quickly, and so forth. But when cues don't work, you have to address the issue head-on.

Awkward? Yes! But if you're kind and matter-of-fact about it, it shouldn't be terribly mortifying for either of you. For example:

- *"I want to explain why I turned down your invitations the last couple of times. I think you're great, and if we didn't work together, you're someone I'd probably like to know socially. But while we work together, the most important thing to me is to be a good manager to you. That means that I need to be able to assess your work impartially and give you feedback, and I don't want you ever to feel that blurred boundaries make it hard for you to approach me if you're unhappy about something. I also don't want anyone else on our team to worry about favoritism. So I want to keep our relationship professional. But I really appreciate you as a colleague and I'm glad to be working with you!"*

29. You've become your friend's boss

My sympathies—this is hard.

When you become your friend's boss, the friendship needs to change. You can still have a warm, friendly relationship, but you can't be friends in the same way anymore. You can't have frequent one-on-one lunches or hang out outside of work or generally maintain the same level of closeness that you might have had. There's now an unequal power dynamic between the two of you, and your job is to judge his work and make decisions that could impact his livelihood.

Even if you're convinced that the two of you can navigate this professionally (and for what it's worth, everyone in this situation believes that until something goes wrong), other people's perceptions matter. As a manager, you can't do things that will create the appearance of favoritism or unequal access.

The best thing you can do is be up-front with your friend so he's not left wondering what's going on. Say something like this:

• *"Hey, I want you to know that since our work relationship has changed, I'm going to have to pull back a bit and have different boundaries, like not going to lunch together so much. I want to make sure that other people don't worry about favoritism, and I don't want you to have to worry about figuring out when I'm your boss and when I'm just a friend. I know this stuff has the potential to be weird, so I wanted to just say it up front and not have you wonder about why I'm suddenly not spending as much time with you. Please don't take it as chilliness—it's just me trying to make sure this works for everyone."*

30. Employee keeps complaining to coworkers but won't bring concerns directly to you

If you have an employee who's constantly grumbling and complaining to coworkers but never brings her complaints to the person who could act on them—you—it's worth saying something. That kind of constant negativity—even if it's low-grade negativity—can wear on other people and poison their environment over time, and it can even be contagious. Plus, if the person has legitimate concerns, those are things you want to hear about and discuss. It helps no one if the employee is grumbling out of your earshot.

Try this:

• *"I think you've gotten into the habit of bringing your concerns about work issues to others on the team rather than to me. If you come to me, I have the chance to try to fix your concerns, or to share things with you that might change your perspective. When you don't come to me and instead vent to others, we both miss that opportunity. Plus, you can end up inadvertently creating a pretty negative atmosphere for others. Going forward, I want to ask you to go to the person with the ability to do something about your complaint—which will often be me—rather than venting to others who can't act on it."*

31. Employee talks too much in meetings

Before you address this one-on-one, it's worth seeing if you can solve the problem by redirecting the person on the spot a few times. If you're able to solve it that way, you can avoid the awkward "You need to talk less" conversation. Here's some language to try:

- *"Quentin, we've heard a lot from you today. Let's hear from people we haven't heard as much from."*

- *"I want to give others a chance to be heard, so let's table that for now."*

- *"I'm going to ask you to hold that for now since we have a lot on our agenda."*

- *"It's a good thought, but I don't want to spend too much more time on this today since we have a lot to get through."*

- *"I'm going to ask Lucinda to jump in here, since she has a lot of experience on this."*

But if that doesn't solve the problem, then it's time to talk to the person privately:

- *"You have valuable input in meetings and you're comfortable speaking up, which is great. But I need to make sure that others have a chance to be heard as well, so I want to ask for your help in ensuring that we're giving others equal airtime."*

- *"When you have a lot to say on a topic, it can be intimidating for others to cut in. I want to ask you to be more aware of how much you're talking in a meeting, and pull back if others aren't getting an equivalent amount of time."* You could add, *"Of course there may be some issues where your role means that you'll have more to say than other people might, but when issues impact the whole group, I want to be sure that we're sharing time more or less evenly."*

- *"I value your input in meetings, but I need to balance that with our need to get through everything on the agenda. Lately we've been having trouble doing that, so I want to ask you to hold off-topic items for the end, if we have time for them, or save them to bring up with me in our one-on-one meetings. Otherwise we end up spending most of the meeting on the first couple of items and never get to the rest."*

Employee is putting magic curses on coworkers

A reader writes:

I work in HR for a school division. I've recently been contacted by a supervisor in our company who has heard that one of his employees, Mandy, has been regularly "cursing" two other employees. By "cursing," I don't mean using foul language. I mean she considers herself something of a witch and has been literally putting curses on these people.

Some background: There are four people on this team, Jeff, Mandy, Whitney, and Roberta. Roberta is leaving, and I met with her today for an exit interview.

I had already become aware that Mandy has, for whatever reasons, decided that she hates Jeff and Whitney. She has been bad-mouthing them to staff, and she bullied Roberta into "joining her" in her hatred. That I can deal with. It has happened before, and I have learned how to deal with workplace bullies and insecure people who feel the need to undermine the reputations of their peers in order to make themselves look better.

What I'm concerned about, and what was confirmed by Roberta during our interview, is this "curse." My information is that Mandy said something along these lines: "When people make me angry, or cross me, I don't worry because I have ways to get rid of them. I've cursed them. I have a place in my house with candles and other items and I know how to do that."

Jeff thinks it is just silly, but Whitney is absolutely terri-

fied. She's looking up ways to ward off curses online and starting to consider going on sick leave because she is afraid to work with this woman. (To make it worse, both Jeff and Whitney got really sick and missed almost a full week of work approximately two weeks after Roberta said that Mandy "cursed" them, which adds to Whitney's fear!)

To me, regardless of whether or not she is Wiccan or a witch or practices voodoo or whatever she does, this is a bona fide threat against another employee. I honestly want to treat this pretty seriously, separate from the bullying issue. Thoughts?

I think that's exactly right—it's intended as a threat and that's not acceptable.

Normally I'm a big fan of managers handling performance problems on their staff themselves rather than looking to HR to do it for them, but in this case, since she's putting curses on her manager, I can see an argument for your having a one-time meeting with her and her manager and jointly laying down the law. (Of course, this may just get you added to the list of people she's cursing, but black magic is one of many occupational hazards.)

When you meet with her, tell her clearly that it's not acceptable to threaten to curse or otherwise harm anyone she works with—and that threatening people with harm, regardless of the means, is grounds for termination. Be clear that this is a one-time warning, and that if it happens again, you'll let her go. And in this same conversation, you should also make it clear that badmouthing her coworkers to others isn't acceptable either, and that she's expected to behave professionally and pleasantly while she's at work. Basically, this is the "Your behavior is far over the bounds of what we will accept here, we take it seriously, and we're going to have zero tolerance for it going forward" conversation.

In addressing this, make sure that you don't get caught up in a long series of warnings to her. Behaving this way is sufficiently unacceptable that it warrants only a single warning and then firing. In fact, frankly, if you're 100 percent sure that the reports you've heard are true, I'd assume that you're going to need to let her go fairly soon, because good employees just don't operate this way (and I'm talking about all of the behavior, not just the curses), and I'm highly skeptical that she's a stellar performer on every other front.

Meanwhile, I would start reading up on counterspells, potions, and hexes, as you're probably going to need them.

32. Employee won't take no for an answer

If you have an employee who doesn't ever seem to hear "no" and keeps pressing for things you've already declined (project assignments, a new office, a raise, or whatever it might be), the kindest thing you can do is be extremely firm and extremely clear—so that the person truly hears the information you're conveying.

For example, if your employee keeps pushing to take on an area of work that you can't or won't assign to her, say something like this:

- *"This has come up several times now, so I want to make sure that I'm being really clear with you. I hear you that you'd like to do more work on our events. But we're fully staffed in that area, and I need you to focus on the job we hired you for, which is bookkeeping. I don't foresee that changing; the bookkeeping work is a full-time job and will continue to be. I hope that's something you can accept and be happy with, because we can't continue to revisit it."*

In most cases, that will solve the problem. But if it doesn't and the person continues to push, then you need to get away from addressing the request and instead address the inappropriate persistence:

- *"I really need you to hear me on this, because you've continued to raise the issue despite my telling you that it's not something we can do. I know that this is important to you, and I've tried to be really transparent with you that it's not something we can do. We can't keep having the same conversation over and over. Knowing that the answer isn't going to change and that we can't keep revisiting this, what makes sense from here?"*

33. Employee overstepped his authority

When an employee does something he isn't authorized to do on his own, the first thing to ask yourself is whether he should reasonably have known not to. Have you been clear with him about the boundaries of his authority and what sorts of things you want to be consulted on? If not, approach it from that angle:

- *"I realized that we never talked about how to handle it when something like this comes up. Dealing with the ethics board is high-stakes, so if there's any further contact with them, on this matter or anything else in the future, I need to be consulted before we respond."*

If there are broader lessons to be drawn as well, mention those, too:

- *"Please come to me first with anything high-stakes—such as legal issues, public statements, or anything dealing with governing boards. I need to sign off on anything we do in those areas before we do it."*

But if you think the employee should have known better, say something like this:

- *"I'm concerned that you spoke to a reporter yesterday rather than sending the call to one of our spokespeople, as our policy directs you to do. What happened there?"*

. . . followed by something like:

- *"I want to be clear that this is a policy we have in place for a reason, and it's important that you follow it. Going forward, if you think there might be a reason to do something that's against our policy, in this area or any other, come talk to me first and get my sign-off. If you just plunge ahead, that can end up being pretty serious."*

34. Employee has a bad attitude

The trick about addressing a bad attitude is to figure out how to articulate specifically what you're seeing that's reading as "bad attitude" to you. That way you can keep the focus on *behaviors,* rather than on how the employee *feels.* Ultimately, it's okay for employees to feel however they want, as long as they're behaving in a way that's aligned with what you need from them.

Plus, once you focus on the problematic behaviors, it will be much easier to address the "bad attitude" issue the same way you would any other performance problem. For example:

- *"When you roll your eyes in meetings and give one-word answers to questions, people think you don't want to be there, and it shuts down conversation. What's going on?"*

- *"Everyone gets frustrated at work occasionally, but when you snap at coworkers or speak rudely to them, it will make people dread working with you. Yesterday, when Miguel asked you for that list of upcoming art exhibits, you sighed loudly and said that he should find it himself. Doing well in this role requires having good relationships with colleagues, and if people are afraid to approach you, it will impact your work and your success."*

- *"I've noticed that you've been making a lot of comments lately about things patients do that annoy you. We all blow off steam now and then, but it's important that we talk about our patients with respect. I'm getting the sense that it's become harder for you to keep up a positive, compassionate attitude lately. Does that resonate with how you're feeling?"*

- *"When you shoot down people's ideas the way you did in yesterday's meeting, it makes people less likely to suggest new ideas in the future. I don't need you to cheerlead for every idea that comes up, and there's value in helping refine ideas and think through potential obstacles. But I'd like you to bring more of a sense of possibility to these discussions and look for ways that we could make something work, rather than defaulting to assuming that we can't."*

35. Communicating a decision from above that you don't agree with

One of the trickiest parts of management is your duty to represent your company's management team to your staff even when you don't agree with their decisions. On the one hand, you have an obligation to your company and your own managers not to undermine their decisions when talking to your staff members. On the other hand, if you appear to be parroting the official line without thought or nuance, you'll lose credibility and create cynicism on your team.

So how do you navigate situations where you need to communicate and/or implement a decision that you don't agree with? The key is to be calm and matter-of-fact and note that there were factors to consider other than your team's own priorities. In some cases, like when your team legitimately worries about unforeseen negative consequences from the decision, it can make sense to agree to raise those concerns again down the road if necessary.

It might sound like this:

- *"This isn't the decision that I would have made, but I know that they had to consider a number of competing factors, and ours weren't the only interests in play."*

- *"I shared our concerns about X and Y, but there were other factors that the company needed to consider as well. Ulti-*

mately, this is the decision they felt made the most sense, given everything that was in play—including concerns outside our group. However, if X or Y does end up causing serious issues for us, I'll ask to revisit it at that point, when we're able to share actual impacts."

36. Employee wants you to promise confidentiality before sharing a concern

Sometimes an employee may ask to talk to you in confidence. It's tempting to immediately agree that you won't share whatever you're told, but doing that can cause problems—because there are some pieces of information that as a manager you'll need to act upon (such as a harassment complaint or information about other serious wrongdoing). And if you promise confidentiality but then can't deliver it, you'll leave employees wary of coming to you in the future.

The better option is to say something like this:

- *"I'll do my best to keep what you tell me off the record, but I want to be transparent that without hearing what you want to say, I can't promise you complete confidentiality. It's possible that I could end up being obligated to share it. But if that happens, I will make sure that you don't suffer any repercussions for coming to me about it."*

That last piece usually gets at what people are worried about, and by addressing that up front, you'll generally assuage most worries.

37. Employee is always pushing back / arguing / undermining your authority

It can be exhausting to have an employee constantly push back on every minor request or decision. As a boss, you don't want to resort to "Because I said so," but you also don't want to have to engage in endless debate.

The way to address it is to name the issue and explain why it's a problem:

- *"Can I give you some feedback about something? I've noticed that you've been pushing back on assignments and decisions really frequently, at least several times a week. I want to know when you have questions about something or ideas about a better way to do it, but I have to balance that with our need to move our work forward and not debate every detail."*

Depending on the sorts of issues that the employee is raising and your willingness to discuss them at some later point, you could also add:

- *"Going forward, I'd like you to hold the things that are more minor, and if they still seem big to you a few weeks later, put them on a list for us to discuss when we have our next one-on-one."* (In many cases, the person will find that many of the items don't seem as important after a few weeks have gone by.)

How do I correct employees about small things?

A reader writes:

I work for a software startup with a typical "relaxed work-place" vibe. I've noticed lately that I suck at managing people who behave in a particular way—presuming that it's okay to do something without asking me, when it actually isn't okay. For example, if someone asks if he can take a break when it's not appropriate, I can easily correct him and set expectations. But if he announces that he's taking a break and then walks off, I freeze and have no idea how to respond.

As these are not always situations that I've anticipated, I want to make sure I'm addressing them fairly while thinking on my feet. I also don't want to say something publicly that could be considered passive-aggressive. Any tips on how to manage these situations better?

Just be matter-of-fact and assert what you need—which, as the manager, you have standing to do, so you don't need to feel weird about it.

If you don't speak up when something is a problem, you're not really doing your job. (That doesn't mean that you always need to get it exactly right in the moment; most normal people can't do that every time, and it's fine to address it later if you miss it in the moment, as long as you do it reasonably soon afterward.)

But the flip side of this is that you don't want to come down on people inappropriately hard, either. What you want is to be comfortable simply stating what you need in a confident, straightforward way. For example:

• If someone announces that he's taking a break at a time that would be disruptive to the work, you can calmly say, "Actually, I need you to finish up X before you go, so maybe in half an hour instead? Thanks!"

• If someone interrupts you in a meeting, you can simply say, "I'd like to finish what I'm saying and then we'll come back to you."

• If someone says "I'm letting the shippers know we're going to need an extra day before we send the file" and that will throw you off schedule, you can say, "I'd like to stick to our original mail date. Tell me what hold-up you're running into, and let's see if we can solve it in a way that doesn't delay the job."

The idea is not to make your "Actually, no" into a big, fraught thing. You're just calmly asserting appropriate authority. You can be perfectly kind and friendly while doing it, as long as you're clear (and, if needed, firm).

Also, keep in mind that in many contexts it should be okay for people to simply let you know what they're doing without asking for permission . . . so be sure that when you object, it's in cases where you really do need to, and not just because you're annoyed on principle that they didn't check with you first. You want to *encourage* independent judgment and decision-making, and you want people to be autonomous to whatever extent their jobs and their professional maturity allow—so if you do feel yourself wanting to step in just on principle, resist that urge!

38. You lost your cool and snapped or yelled at someone

Even the best managers can find themselves so frustrated that they lose their cool and snap at an employee—or, worse, yell.

If you find yourself embarrassed about how you behaved with an employee, chances are that you should apologize. Managers sometimes hesitate to apologize for their own behavior, fearing that it will make them look weak. But admitting that you were wrong and taking responsibility for it is likely to increase people's respect for you (as long as you're not flipping out and yelling at people every day; more on that in a minute). Say it this way:

- *"I want to apologize to you for my tone when we spoke yesterday. I was concerned that we were off course from the plan we'd agreed to, but that's not an excuse for snapping at you. I respect you and your work, and I'm sorry if that didn't come through."*

An important note: Regularly snapping or yelling at employees will severely damage your staff's morale and impede your effectiveness. If you find yourself guilty of this, take a look at what's causing it—whether it's your own stress level, a problem with an employee that you need to address differently, or something else.

39. You realize you were wrong about a policy or decision

Life as a manager gets much easier when you realize that you don't actually need to be infallible (and, frankly, *can't* be infallible). You're going to make mistakes and occasionally call things the wrong way, and that's okay. The important thing is to be transparent about it when it happens, because that's what builds trust and credibility with your staff and others around you. For example:

- *"I want to be up-front that I think I made the wrong call on the X project. I've taken another look at the strategy, and I'm convinced that Raquel and Ashra were right when they advocated Y from the start. So we're going to do Y, and I want to own up to calling this one wrong."*

- *"I appreciate you all working with me to implement the new policy on time off. Now that we've had a few months to see it play out, I'm realizing that it's not addressing our scheduling needs as well as I'd hoped it would. Rather than stick to something that isn't working well, I want to recognize that reality and return to our old policy while I continue to try to figure out if there's a better way to address this. And I welcome ideas for better ways to combat the scheduling crunch from anyone who has them!"*

- *"I want to apologize for asking you to work late last week. I had thought that we needed to have the X project out the door by the next day and I hadn't anticipated the delay that we ran into. I know you canceled your plans to make that deadline, and I'm grateful that you did—and sorry that it turned out not to be needed."*

40. You catch an employee in a lie

I once managed someone who told me that she'd sent an important email to a vendor when I was 99 percent sure from the context that she hadn't. Because this wasn't the first time I'd doubted her veracity, I said this to her: "If I'm wrong about this, I'm going to apologize profusely . . . but can you show me in your computer where that sent email is so we can look at it together?" There was a long, uncomfortable pause, and then she confessed there was no email.

In that case, I ended up firing the employee because that was the last straw in a string of problems. Firing someone won't be warranted every time, but it's important that when you catch someone lying, you address it. Someone who thinks it's okay to operate that way is someone you can't trust or rely on, and you have to be able to trust people in order to continue working together.

If you catch an employee in a lie that *isn't* job-ending, say something like this:

- *"I'm very concerned that you told me that Olive knew you'd be out yesterday and was fine with covering for you, when she actually didn't know anything about it. What happened?"*

Assuming that the person doesn't respond with an explanation that clears everything up, you'd then say something like this:

- *"I need to be able to rely on what you say to me and trust that it's correct. If I can't do that, I'd need to second-guess everything you say, and that's not good for either of us. You've always done good work here, so I'm willing to give you the benefit of the doubt that this was a one-time lapse in judgment. But I want to be really clear how essential it is that I be able to trust what you tell me in the future."*

41. Employee's (or job candidate's) parent contacts you

One weird result of the trend toward more involved parenting has been the inappropriate overinvolvement of some parents in their kids' work lives, like calling employers on their behalf to ask "Why didn't you hire my kid?" or "Can you please approve Imogen's time off request for our family vacation?" If you're thinking "No way" because this is obviously a ridiculous thing for a parent to do, it's really something that has started happening in recent years. I even once had an employee's mom—a lawyer—contact me on her law firm's letterhead to complain about a work issue her daughter was facing. (It turned out the daughter hadn't reported the facts correctly to her mom.)

If this happens to you, you don't need to play along. In fact, you shouldn't—it's important for these parents to hear that what they're doing isn't appropriate. You can and should refuse to talk to them about their kid, and explain why:

- *"I only discuss performance ratings with employees themselves. This isn't something I'm willing to discuss with an outside party."*

- *"I'm certainly willing to talk to your son about why we rejected his application if he contacts me directly. But we don't talk to third parties about that kind of thing."*

To either of these, you could also add:

- *"For what it's worth, this kind of call reflects poorly on your son and could really harm his professional reputation, so I urge you not to intervene in his work life in the future."*

42. Employee is drinking too much at office social events

Office social events can be tricky; they're social, so people let down their guard more than they otherwise might at work, but they're still work events with potentially serious ramifications for people's work reputations and relationships.

If you have an employee who drinks too much at office social events, you have an obligation to speak to the person (both for the person's own sake and for the comfort of her coworkers).

Start with something like this:

- *"At a few happy hours recently, you seemed more than a little tipsy. Everything okay?"*

It's possible that you'll hear something that will make the next part of the conversation less necessary—maybe the person was adjusting to a new medication, or has already realized that she overdid it and vowed not to let it happen again. But you want to start by asking, so that you're not launching into a lecture that doesn't quite fit the context.

But assuming that you don't hear anything like that, the next thing to say is:

- *"You were being pretty aggressive with others who were there, and you said some things to Matilda that I don't think you would have said if you were sober. Going for-ward, I want you to watch your alcohol intake at work events, and limit yourself to one or two drinks at most. You do great work and I don't want overindulging to impact your reputation or your relationships with colleagues."*

Our receptionist won't stop hugging people

A reader writes:
We have a gregarious receptionist who regularly solicits hugs from people—not from other employees but from outside frequent visitors and volunteers who come into the office.

Most often, this happens when someone first arrives, usually with people she knows but hasn't seen in several days. But I have also seen her approach a visiting guest speaker whom she had never met before with a hug, so I was a bit surprised by that.

These are not simple polite hugs of greeting but rather demonstrative productions. She also does it in a way that draws a lot of attention to herself—for example, she'll some-times go for a longer-than-necessary, full-body hug. I'm not sure how else to describe it. She has a naturally loud voice, so even if I'm in another room, I can usually overhear the accompanying expressions. She'll loudly announce how good it feels to be hugged. It just seems overly self-

indulgent and unnecessary. I'm not trying to be judgmental, but I know that others have expressed discomfort with it.

Some people have directly told her that they do not hug, but others seem to tolerate or accept it, while others seem completely fine with it. But at least one person has complained to me that it's very unprofessional.

I will have to do a performance review with her in the future and would like to address the topic then. I intend to give this employee a clear recommendation that she scale it back significantly. But where is the line, exactly, in something like this?

I'm not sure I can say exactly where the line is—but it's somewhere far, far away from where this employee has ended up. It's not that hugging someone is never appropriate in an office—there *are* offices where the occasional hug occurs—but it certainly shouldn't be the default mode of greeting someone. Regardless of where the line is for normal people, though, your employee has shown an inability to judge when it is and isn't appropriate, so it just needs to stop entirely.

Don't wait for her performance evaluation to talk to her—do it now. Performance evaluations shouldn't have surprises in them; you should be giving people feedback throughout the year. It's not fair to blindside someone in a review, and it's also not good management to neglect problems until then. (I know that it sometimes feels easier to wait for the formal evaluation, but that would be abdicating your responsibility as her manager.)

Say something like this: "I really appreciate how friendly you are to visitors to the office. However, not everyone is comfortable with being hugged in a professional environment, so I need you to stop that. It's true that some people *are* comfortable with it, but others aren't, and people in the second group won't always speak up because they don't want to create awkwardness. I know your intention is to be welcoming, but different people have different physical boundaries, and in an office, we need to err on the side of making sure no one feels uncomfortable. So that means no more hugging."

And you need to be very direct about this. Don't be tempted to just tell her to "scale back the hugging" or "limit it to people you know," because she's already shown that she doesn't have appropriate judgment in this area and can't tell when someone would or wouldn't be comfortable with it.

If she continues to argue, you can simply say, "Be that as it may, no more hugging going forward."

But talk to her now—don't wait. I can almost guarantee you that some people who need to visit your office are dreading it because of the unwelcome physical embrace they know they'll receive.

43. Asking your staff not to buy you holiday gifts

If you're a manager, it can be uncomfortable to receive gifts from employees. Because of the power dynamic, people can feel obligated to purchase gifts when they don't want to or can't afford to, and that's especially true if they see their co-workers getting gifts for the boss. But it can be tricky to figure out how to discourage your staff from giving you gifts without feeling presumptuous (maybe they weren't planning to give you a gift anyway!) or Scrooge-like. Here are two options:

- *"I know this is the season of office gift-giving, so I want to say up front that simply doing your jobs well is enough of a gift for me. Please spend your money on your family or yourself, and know that I'm incredibly grateful to have a staff like you."*

- *"I don't want to assume anyone is thinking of getting me a gift, but just in case you might be, I want to say that while that's very kind of you, please put that money toward your family and friends instead."*

And of course, say something early enough that you can preempt any gift buying (or angst about gift buying). The beginning of December is usually good timing.

However, if you receive a gift from an employee anyway, you should accept it graciously (assuming it's not extravagantly expensive). You don't want to make people feel bad, which is the likely outcome if you refuse to accept a small gift on principle. Instead, the idea is to ensure that your staff don't feel *obligated* to use their money to buy things for you.

44. How to address problems you heard about secondhand

When you hear reports of a problem that you haven't observed firsthand, ideally you'd find ways to try to observe it yourself. (For example, if you hear that an employee keeps leaving work early, you could make a point of stopping by her office close to quitting time.) But that's not always possible: You might work across the country from each other, or the person might behave differently around you than around coworkers. Or the problem might be serious enough that you can't wait to try to observe it happening again (like yelling at a client).

When you need to act on something that you know about only secondhand, the most important thing is that you not assume that what you heard was true or that you have the full story. It might be true and you might have the full story, but starting with that assumption when you don't know for sure is unfair to your employee. Say something like this:

- *"I don't normally like to rely on secondhand reports, but sometimes there's no way around it. I've heard that you might have lost your temper with Karen and Jamal the other day. I know I might not have the full story, so I wanted to ask you what happened."*

45. Telling an employee he didn't get a promotion

When you have to tell someone that he didn't get a promotion he was hoping for, the best thing you can do is be as honest and straightforward as you can about the reasons, let the employee know that he's valued, and talk about what, if anything, he could do to be a stronger candidate for a promotion in the future.

Here's what it might sound like:

- *"I want to let you know that we've made a decision about the communications director position, and we've decided to offer it to an outside candidate. I know this is probably disappointing news, so I wanted to tell you in person and explain a bit about the reasoning. You have really great relationships with reporters, and a particular talent for thinking up creative ways to get our message into the news.*

The area where you were less strong was in managing a team. We ended up going with a candidate with more ex-perience managing a team of this size, because doing that well will be so crucial for the role. That said, I've never seen anyone grow in this role as quickly as you have in the last year. And the contributions that you're making to our media presence are huge; you're a big part of the reason that we had as much success this year as we did. I want to make sure that there's a path for growth for you here, and I'm planning to talk to the new director about creating ways for you to get more management experience so that the next time a promotion opens up, you'll be better positioned for it. We can talk about that more whenever you want, but for now I wanted to let you know the decision."

Of course, if the reality is that there isn't likely to be much of a path for promotion for the person, be honest about that! For example, you might say something like this:

• *"I want to be up-front with you that because we're such a small staff, there's not a whole lot of opportunity to move up from this role. The jobs above this one all require pretty senior-level media experience, and unfortunately we don't have a way to get you that experience. I know that means that in order to move up, you'll need to leave us at some point, and I'll support you however I can when that time comes. But in the meantime, you're a hugely valuable part of our work here, and I hope we'll get to keep you around for a while before that happens."*

46. Turning down a request for a raise

Can you turn down an employee's request for a raise without destroying the person's morale? In many cases, yes, as long as you handle it the right way. Here's how:

1. **Hear the person out.** Even if your initial (private) response is that a raise would be totally unwarranted, it's useful to know why she thinks she deserves one—and you want her to feel that you gave her a fair hearing. So if the person hasn't already explained her reasoning, say this:

- *"Tell me more about what you're thinking and why."*

2. **Ask for some time to consider the request.** Even if you're still confident that you shouldn't grant the raise, it's smart to ask for time to consider it. You might find that sitting with the request for a while actually does change your thinking, but even if not, you want your employee to see that you gave it real consideration. But don't take too long—you don't want to leave the person hanging, especially if the answer is likely to be no. Say something like this:

- *"I appreciate your raising this, and I'd like to take some time to consider it. I'm going to give it some thought and will get back to you by the end of this week."*

3. **Once you think it over, if the answer is still no, explain your reasoning.** Be as straightforward as you can. For example:

- *"I've taken a look at how your salary compares with the salaries of other people here and in the market more broadly. Based on that, I believe you're paid competitively for the role."* (If you consulted with HR on salary data, be sure to mention that as well.)

- *"We've talked in the last few months about areas I'd like you to work on approaching differently, such as taking more initiative on projects and having clearer communication with colleagues. You've gotten a good start on tackling those, but I'd like to see sustained improvement there before we revisit your salary."*

- *"I think you made a good case for a raise. Your work has been excellent, and you're right that your responsibilities have increased. The reality is that we just don't have the cash flow to say yes right now, especially with the budget shortfall."*

4. **Explain what it would take to get a "yes" in the future.** For example:

- *"One path to a raise in the future would be to take on more paralegal work. If that's something that interests you, we could put together a plan to start getting you more experience in that area."*

- *"If you show me over the next six months that you've made significant progress in the areas we've talked about focusing on, I'd be glad to take another look at your salary then."*

- *"This is just about the budget, not about whether you deserve it. You're at the top of my list to revisit this as soon as we get more breathing room in the budget."*

47. Warning someone that his job is in jeopardy

If you have serious concerns about an employee's performance or behavior, and those concerns could conceivably lead to your letting that person go at some point in the future, you must, must, *must* tell the person *now*. Too often, managers don't give a clear warning, and as a result, the person ends up blindsided when he loses his job. Ironically, managers who shy away from giving this kind of clear warning are usually avoiding it because it feels like an unkind message to deliver . . . but it's *so* much more unkind to deny someone the chance to know how serious your concerns are.

So you must say it. If you're like most people, it will be a hard conversation, and you will be very tempted to soften your language. But it's crucial that you don't; you need to be very explicit so the message isn't lost. Here's one way to do it:

- *"I'm hopeful that you'll be able to make the improvements we've talked about. But I want to be transparent with you that these issues are serious enough that they could jeopardize your job here. That said, I'm committed to working with you to help get your work to where we need it, and I hope that we can make it work."*

Or, when you're ready to commit to a timeline for resolving the situation:

- *"I'm hopeful that you'll be able to make the improvements we've talked about. But I want to be transparent with you that these issues are serious enough that if you're not able to show strong progress over the next month, I will need to let you go. But I'm ready to work with you however I can over the next month to help get your work to where we need it to be, and I'm hopeful that we'll be able to."*

48. Letting someone go

Firing an employee is one of the hardest things that managers do. It's also one of the most important, because you'll never accomplish as much as you otherwise could if you don't address performance problems head-on. Plus, keeping low performers around is terrible for the morale of the rest of your staff (as you probably know if you've ever worked with someone who didn't pull her weight).

The most important thing to know about what to say when letting someone go is that in 99 percent of cases, the firing shouldn't come as a surprise. It should be the final installment in a conversation that's been ongoing, one in which you've talked about the problems, talked about what needs to change, and been honest that lack of improvement could result in your having to let the person go. If you've done that, then the actual firing conversation should sound like this:

- *"When we talked two weeks ago, we discussed the fact that if you didn't meet the benchmarks we had laid out, we wouldn't be able to keep you on. Unfortunately, although I know you have been trying, we're now at that point and have decided to let you go."*

If you weren't *quite* that clear previously—for example, if you talked about the problems but didn't give a specific timeline—say this (and vow to be more transparent in the future!):

- *"We've been talking for the past few months about the changes that I needed to see in your work. I know that*

you've been trying, but unfortunately I haven't seen the im-
provements that I needed. I think ultimately this just isn't
the right match between your talents and what we need,
and we've decided to let you go."

The next thing to cover is logistics, because the person is likely wondering exactly what this means, such as whether she's supposed to leave immediately or work out the rest of the day or week, whether you'll pay any severance, and so forth. So address those concerns proactively:

- *"Today will be your last day, and you're free to leave after this meeting. You don't need to worry about wrapping up any loose ends with your work. We'll pay you through the end of the month. And if there are things you need to get from your desk, you can either do that right now or I can send them to you, if you'd prefer not to have to deal with that now. Do you have any questions about logistics that I can answer for you?"*

A few important notes:

- **Deliver the decision early in the conversation.** Don't try to ease into the news or soften the blow, or you risk the person's not realizing that the decision has been made and that it's final. You don't want her sitting there thinking that this is just another feedback conversation or trying to sway your assessment.

- **Keep the conversation relatively short.** You've made your decision, and this shouldn't be a debate. Let the person know the decision, say that you appreciated her efforts (if that's the case), and then cover logistics.

- **Throughout the conversation, you want your tone to be kind and compassionate.** It's okay to acknowledge that you're sorry this is the outcome.

49. Telling your team that you've fired someone

Telling your team that you've fired someone can be tricky. In some cases, everyone will have seen it coming, agree that it needed to be done, and be relieved that you addressed the situation. In other cases, people might feel blindsided, since it's not always obvious to coworkers when someone is struggling with his work. When people feel blindsided, it can cause drama and angst (because you'll get people speculating about what happened, and some people will wonder if they, too, need to worry about being fired).

At the same time, you want to protect the fired person's privacy and dignity to the extent that you can, so in most cases the reasons for the firing should be on a need-to-know basis.

The thing that will help most here is to be open with your staff about how you address performance problems *in general*. Let them know that people are clearly warned and given a chance to improve before being let go (except for egregious situations like embezzling or punching a coworker). If people understand that you don't make arbitrary or unfair personnel decisions and that they'll know it if their jobs are ever in jeopardy, there's likely to be a lot less drama around firings.

So what do you actually say when you need to share news that you've let someone go? You can start with a pretty light-on-details message, as long as you're clear about the basics. For example:

- *"Today was Clea's last day, and we wish her the best. We're going to launch a search for a replacement right away, but until that person is hired, Jordan will be temporarily handling her projects."*

If you're pressed for more details after that, you can say something like this:

- *"I want to respect Clea's privacy, but yes, we let her go. I know that when that happens, it can feel surprising to the person's coworkers, who might not have known there were problems, but I want to stress that it's not something that would have come as a surprise to the person herself. When we make the decision to let someone go, it's generally after multiple conversations with the person about what the issues are and chances to show improvement. So I want to be sure you know that except in very egregious situations, it's not something that would ever come out of the blue."*

50. Telling your team you're leaving

When you tell your team that you're leaving your job, the first and biggest question on their minds is going to be what it means for them. Is a new boss coming in who's going to change everything? How long will they be without a manager? How will things work in the interim?

You might not have the answers to all—or any—of these questions, but you should be prepared to tell them *something*, even if it's just the timeline for figuring out the answers. Here's how it might sound:

- *"I have some bittersweet news to share. I've made the difficult decision to leave my job here and accept a position* managing communications for another firm. I'm excited about the new job, but sad to be leaving all of you! You've been wonderful to work with—I'll miss our work here and you personally, and I'm looking forward to staying in touch. I know you probably have a lot of questions about what this means for the department. We're in the process of figuring out all the details, but I can tell you that I'll be here through the end of the month, and my top priority will be helping to get interim management in place so that things keep running smoothly. We'll also be looking to bring in a new permanent person to fill my role, and I'll share details on that process as soon as I know more."

CHAPTER 4

Conversations with Your Job Interviewer

Job interviews probably have the strangest and most obvious power dynamics of any of the conversations in this book—or at least they feel that way to most people. It's common to feel that your interviewer holds all the power and you're supposed to simply wait to receive her judgment.

And sure, your interviewer is indeed assessing you—for an interviewer, that's the point of the conversation. But it's not a one-way street; you should be assessing your interviewer (and the company, and the job) right back. Just as much as your interviewer is there to figure out if you're the best match for the job, you're there to figure out if the job is the best match for you.

That doesn't mean there aren't some power dynamics in interviews that you need to play along with. There are, and they usually come in the form of double standards. For instance, it's considered okay for your interviewer to answer a call in midinterview, but it would be a pretty shocking breach for you to do that. Your interviewer can get away with being a bit late (although not hours late), while you're expected to be precisely on time. That's just how the conventions on this process have shaped up.

But when it comes to interview power dynamics, the thing to remember is that your interviewer isn't doing you a *favor*. This is a business conversation, and your interviewer is hoping that you will be the solution to a business problem (the job vacancy). You're there for a business reason too—to determine whether you'd like to enter into a business arrangement with this employer—and you should handle it the same way you would any other business conversation.

That means that you should:

• Expect to be treated with a reasonable amount of consideration (and not, for example, be left waiting for two hours before your interviewer shows up, or have your interview canceled at the last minute without profuse apologies).

• Remember to assess whether you want the job and whether you would be good at it. Don't let that get lost in your focus on getting the offer.

• Ask the questions that you need answered in order to determine if this is a job that you'd want, in a culture you want, working with and for people you'd want to work with and for.

• Feel free to assert yourself if you're being treated poorly.

• Be candid if you decide that the job isn't for you.

Once you realize the interviewer doesn't hold *all* the cards, you'll come across as a more confident and appealing candidate, and you'll probably find interviews much less stressful, too.

With that groundwork laid, let's look at some of the trickier conversations that you might need to have in this process, and how to handle them.

1. You're called out of the blue for a phone interview you weren't expecting

Smart employers schedule phone interviews in advance, but there are plenty who will call you up and try to interview you on the spot without any warning.

If it's a good time for you, if you're in a reasonably quiet place where you're not likely to be interrupted, and if you don't have to dart out the door in ten minutes, then great—maybe you're comfortable doing the interview then and there. But if those things aren't true—if you're in the check-out line at a grocery store, or you just woke up, or you're in the middle of an open office with coworkers all around you—it's okay to explain that you can't talk at the moment and ask to reschedule:

- *"I'd love to talk, but I'm at work right now and heading into a meeting. Is there a time later today or tomorrow when I could call you back?"*

- *"I'm glad to hear from you. I'm not in a spot right now where I can easily talk. Is there a time later today or tomorrow when I could call you back?"*

2. You're going to be late to your interview

Ideally, you'd never be late to an interview and would always arrive with plenty of time to spare, the picture of calm. But if disaster strikes and you realize that you're going to be late,

call the employer as soon as you know, give your best estimate of when you'll arrive, and be *extremely* apologetic.

The thing to keep in mind here is that the interviewer
doesn't know you and has no way of knowing if this is highly
out of character for you or if you're someone who's going to
be late all the time once you're on the job. Because of that,
the way you handle the situation will carry a ton of weight,
so it's crucial to make it clear that this isn't your normal M.O.
You can do that by sounding mortified and making it clear
that you take the lateness seriously.

For example, when you call to explain that you're going to
be late, you could say this:

- *"I'm so sorry—I gave myself plenty of extra time, but there's
  a huge traffic jam on Route 45 that will probably make me
  about twenty minutes late. Will that still work for your
  schedule? I of course understand if it won't."*

Then, when you arrive, apologize again:

- *"I'm so sorry about being late. I'm neurotic about punctu-
  ality, so this is pretty mortifying to me."*

That may seem like a lot of apologizing for something that
can happen to anyone—but again, it goes back to the fact
that they don't know you yet and don't know what your normal habits are.

3. There's a mistake on your résumé

Of course you want your résumé to be flawlessly polished,
but you are human, and it's possible that something on it is
wrong. Maybe you got the dates of your last job wrong, or

the last line somehow dropped off the page completely and now it appears you never attended school, or you wrote that you graduated in 1912 rather than 2012.

First, know that if you got an interview, the employer couldn't have been too put off—and may not have even spotted the error. Still, though, it's smart to address it up front, both so that you can demonstrate that you aren't oblivious to it and so that you can correct the information. (Plus, you'll give your interviewer a chance to see you gracefully handling an awkward situation, which is not a bad thing.)

Here's what it might sound like:

- *"Before we get started, I want to mention that I saw that somehow the version of my résumé that I sent you cut off the portion about my education. Here's a version that includes it."*

- *"Before we get started, I should note that despite what my résumé says, I did not actually graduate in 1912. It should say 2012. I'm normally a neurotic proofreader, so this is mortifying. And I hope you aren't disappointed that I'm not a centenarian."*

Now, what if you didn't notice the error and the interviewer brings it to your attention? In that case, try something like this:

- *"Oh, no! Thank you for bringing that to my attention so I can fix it. I'm normally a neurotic proofreader, so this is mortifying."*

4. You don't understand an interview question

If you don't fully understand a question in your interview, don't try to bluff; simply ask your interviewer to clarify the question. Say any of these:

- *"Could I ask you to repeat the question?"*

- *"I want to make sure I'm understanding. Are you asking ____ (restate in your own words)?"*

- *"I'm not sure I'm completely following what you're asking and I want to make sure I give you the answer you're looking for. Can you put it a different way?"*

5. You're stumped by an interview question

If you're totally stumped by an interview question, the worst thing you can do is to try to bluff your way through it. If the question is an important one, the interviewer is going to be able to tell you're bluffing, and that's not good. Instead, be up-front about it. You'll come across as having more integrity, and good interviewers will appreciate seeing you handle the situation with grace.

What to say depends on the type of question you were asked. If it's a question about your knowledge of something, be honest that you don't know and then talk about how you'd go about finding the answer:

- *"Hmm, you know, I actually don't know the answer to that! When I've encountered similar things in the past, I've done X and Y and that usually gets me pointed in the right direction."*

On the other hand, if the question is more along the lines of "Tell me about a time when you had to do X" and you can't think of a good example to share, just be straightforward about that. Then, ideally, you'd either share an example of something related although not identical, or talk about how you think you'd approach the situation if it occurred. For example:

- *"It's a good question. I'm having trouble thinking of a time when I've encountered that at work. But if it did come up, I'd approach it this way . . ."*

6. Company has terrible online reviews from employees

If you're interviewing with a company that has terrible reviews on a site like Glassdoor or otherwise has reputation problems, you might be wondering if there's any way to ask about it in your interview.

As long as you bring up the topic professionally, it's a perfectly legitimate thing to ask about. You're considering tying yourself to this company for the next few years, so you shouldn't let fears of awkwardness stand in the way of getting your concerns addressed.

The key is to frame it in a way that doesn't set your interviewer on the defensive. So your tone should be collaborative rather than accusatory; you want to sound as if you're giving them the benefit of the doubt (even if secretly you're not). For example:

- *"I noticed that the company's reviews from employees on Glassdoor frequently include concerns about culture and work hours. I'm curious what your take is on those issues and whether they're something the company is working to change."*

7. You're getting conflicting information about the job from different interviewers

Talking to multiple people throughout an interview process can be a huge benefit because you can get different perspectives on the job, the culture, the challenges of the role, and so forth. But if you notice that you're hearing different things about key elements of the role—like what the job's focus will be or what's most important for the person to achieve in the first year—it's important to clarify what's going on. Otherwise you risk ending up in a job that is different from what you were signing up for, or where no one can agree on how your success should be measured.

How to say it:

- *"I've heard different perspectives on the job from Anna, Fergus, and Portia. It sounds as if some people want to see the role focus on expanding the training curriculum and some people want to see it focus on bringing in new business. Can you help me get a better sense of how those will be balanced, and whether there's internal alignment about what people want to see from the position?"*

8. Interviewer asks about your religion, ethnicity, plans for children, or other inappropriate topics

Contrary to widespread belief, it's not illegal in the United States for an interviewer to ask you about your religion, ethnicity, marital status, number of children, or plans for kids. However, it's illegal for an employer to make a hiring decision based on your answers to these questions, and therefore smart employers don't ask them. And understandably, encountering these questions makes job seekers nervous—since it raises the specter that the interviewer might discriminate against you in some illegal way.

But that message hasn't reached everyone, and you may encounter an interviewer who asks one of these questions anyway. Sometimes even interviewers who know better do it as part of making small talk (not thinking about how, in the context, it might freak you out).

So what do you do if you encounter this kind of question in an interview?

If it truly seems like the question is being asked as part of making small talk—that your interviewer is just trying to be friendly and build rapport—you'll usually get a better outcome by answering in that spirit.

But if you get the sense that the interviewer is, say, asking whether you're married out of concern that you'll want time off soon to have babies, or is asking what church you go to because she doesn't want to hire any godless heathens, that's a different situation. In that case, here are some options:

- **Address what you think the interviewer's concern really is.** For example, if you think an interviewer is concerned that having kids means that you won't be at work reliably, say this:

- *"There's nothing in my personal life that would interfere with my ability to work the hours needed and make the job a top priority."*

- **Ask why the interviewer is asking.** You have to do this carefully, because if you seem adversarial, the interview will likely never get back on track, but try saying one of these pleasantly and with a tone of genuine curiosity:

  - *"Why do you ask?"*

  - *"I've never been asked that before in an interview. What makes you ask?"*

9. Interviewer takes you to lunch at a restaurant with nothing on the menu you can eat

Interviews over lunch can be tricky under the best of circumstances. But when you have dietary restrictions—you're vegetarian, kosher, gluten intolerant, or so forth—they can have a whole new layer of challenge to them.

Ideally, if you have dietary restrictions, you'd mention them as soon as you learn that your interview will take place over lunch. For example:

- *"That sounds great! I should mention that I'm vegetarian, in case it affects where we go. It's pretty easy to find something vegetarian at most places these days, but I thought I should mention it just in case."*

- Or if you want to discourage the lunch idea: *"I really appreciate the invitation to lunch! I keep kosher, though, and it can be tough to find a kosher restaurant around here. It's so kind of you to offer, but it might be easier to skip lunch for that reason, if that works on your end."*

But what if lunch was sprung on you with no warning and you find yourself walking into a restaurant where it's clear you won't be able to eat anything?

If your interviewer is an even halfway decent person, he will be mortified when he realizes the situation and will want to fix it for you. But the earlier you speak up, the easier that will be. For example:

- *"I should have mentioned this when we walked in, but I figured there would be something on the menu I can eat. But it looks like all they serve is seafood, which I'm allergic to. I'd be happy just to order a beverage if that's okay, or would you prefer to go somewhere else close by?"*

I threw up on the floor during an interview

A reader writes:
I recently had an interview with a company about a position that I was excited about. I was just getting over being sick when I scheduled the interview, so I pushed it back a couple days just to be safe. On the day of the interview, I still had an intermittent cough, but overall I felt fine.

Toward the end of the interview, which was going well, I ended up having a coughing fit, with a deep dry cough that would not go away. The interviewer got up and showed me to the water cooler and told me to take my time, being very nice about it. However, I ended up coughing so hard and so deep I threw up on the floor a little bit, right in front of the interviewer.

I did not know what to do, so I said something to the effect of "Well, that just happened," apologized, and asked where they kept the cleaning supplies. He said not to worry about it, wished me good health, and promptly showed me to the door. Is there any chance of recovery here? Should I call them and apologize?

Oh, no! This is not your fault at all, but I can only imagine how horrified you were. For what it's worth, only a jerk would hold this against you. People get sick, and they sometimes get sick at inopportune times.

I wouldn't call to apologize, but in your post-interview thank-you, in addition to building on points covered in the interview, you could also say something like, "Thank you again for your gracious response when I got ill—that was basically the last thing I'd ever want to happen in an interview." (Personally, I would add, "At least we now both have an interviewing horror story that can top anyone else's," but that may or may not fit your style.)

10. Your interviewer is an hour late

As a job candidate, you probably know that you can't show up even ten minutes late for an interview—but interviewers themselves regularly run behind schedule. It's annoying and unfair, and it's very much the reality of interviews.

Nonetheless, as the candidate, you can certainly judge your interviewer and draw your own conclusions from her behavior. And while being ten minutes late shouldn't be a big deal, being an hour late is truly rude and can be an indicator of serious chaos and disorganization that you might prefer not to work in.

The best way to figure out if your hour-late interviewer is an inconsiderate or disorganized manager or whether there were one-time extenuating circumstances is to pay attention to how the interviewer talks about the delay. Does she seem mortified, apologize profusely, and explain that's not how they do things there? Or does she seem cavalier about making you wait?

If you're having trouble getting a sense of this, you can politely force the interviewer to address the delay by asking this:

- *"I'd thought we'd scheduled for two o'clock—I hope I didn't get the time wrong?"*

If that doesn't prompt a sincere apology, you'll have just learned a lot about your prospective employer.

11. Explaining a long period of unemployment

You may have heard that employers often prefer job candidates who are already employed, and while there can be truth to that, you shouldn't let it freak you out. If you have a long period of unemployment in your recent past, address the work gap concisely, without sounding like you think it's something shameful.

What you say will depend on the reason for the gap, but here are some different ways to talk about it:

- *"I was dealing with a health issue that has since been resolved."* (This is a very handy line, because most employers won't pry for more details. Also, that last part is important, because you're reassuring the employer that you're ready for work again.)

- *"I was caring for a sick family member, but I'm now ready and eager to get back to full-time work."*

- *"Working on a political campaign means intense hours for months on end! So when the campaign ended, I took some time off to relax and think about what I wanted to do next."*

- *"When I left my last job, I was lucky enough to be in a position where I didn't need to find another job right away. So I spent a few months traveling and thinking about what I want to do next, and I'm taking my time and being very selective about the jobs I apply for. I'm interested in this one because . . ."*

- *"I took a couple of years off from accounting after having my daughter, but I'm itching to return to work. When I found myself reading about tax law changes as a leisure activity, I knew it was time to get back to work."*

12. Explaining a past firing

If you were fired from a fairly recent job, you're probably dreading being asked about it in an interview. But lots of people get fired and go on to find plenty of work in the future! Being fired is not the kiss of death for your career.

The keys to talking about a firing with your interviewer are:

- **Be calm.** Make sure that you don't sound defensive or bitter, because if the situation still sounds emotional for you, that's going to be a red flag for your interviewer. You want to sound as if you've learned from what happened and have moved forward.

- **Be concise.** This is crucial! Your interviewer is really only looking for a few sentences about what happened, not expecting a detailed account of what went down.

- **Practice your answer ahead of time.** Firing can be awkward to talk about. Practicing out loud makes it more likely that you won't sound horribly uncomfortable when it comes up.

As for the answer itself, try to sum up in a sentence or two why you and your employer were mismatched or otherwise what went wrong, followed by a sentence about what you've learned or do differently now as a result. For example:

- *"Actually, I was let go. I reported to two different VPs and was getting conflicting instructions from each, and I didn't speak up about it when I should have. I tried to make it all work, which wasn't realistic, and ultimately I dropped some balls. It taught me a lot about needing to speak up early when priorities aren't clear so that that never happens again."*

- *"I was fired. That's on me—I took a job with a heavy coding component, and I'm not an experienced coder. I thought I'd be able to get up to speed quickly enough, but I underestimated how much I'd need to learn. They made the right call, and I was relieved to be able to go back to focusing on design work."*

- *"It ended up being a bad fit. They were looking for design expertise when I'm really a copywriter, not a designer. Ultimately we agreed that it didn't make sense for me to be in that role."*

13. Explaining why you want to change jobs when the real reason is that your boss is crazy but you know you can't say that

I'm normally a huge proponent of being honest in job interviews, since it's the easiest way to make sure that you end up in a job that's actually the right fit for you. If you misrepresent yourself, your experience, or your skills, you can end up in a job that you'll be miserable in or even get fired from.

However, "Why are you leaving your current job?" and "Why did you leave your last job?" are often exceptions to that rule, if the reason you're leaving, or left, is because of a terribly toxic work culture or horrible coworkers or because your boss was bat-shit insane.

The deal is this: It's totally fine if that's the real reason you're leaving. Interviewers know that terrible jobs, bosses, cultures, and coworkers exist. The problem is that you can't generally say it. On the interviewer side of things, if I hear something like that, I'll certainly allow for the possibility that it's accurate—but because I don't know you, I also have to wonder whether *you* were the problem. Is your boss really a micromanager, or do you require a ton of oversight? Were your coworkers truly horrible, or are you hard to get along with? Were things really as bad as you're saying, or are you a prima donna who's going to be impossible to please here, too? Because I don't know you, I have to wonder if your boss's side of the story might be very different.

Plus, frankly, the interviewing convention is simply that you don't bad-mouth a previous employer, and you demonstrate that you know how to conduct yourself reasonably discreetly in business situations.

So where does that leave you? With answers like this:

- *"I'm ready to take on a new challenge! I was originally brought in to launch a new training program, and I've spent the last three years getting that up and running. We launched about eighteen months ago and have already exceeded our sales goals and won an industry award. Now that it's running smoothly, I'm excited to move on to a new project."*

- *"I've been able to learn a huge amount in my current role and have taken on responsibilities like X and Y. But I'm really interested in moving into Z, and since we're a small team, there's not a lot of room for me to do that in my current role. That's why I'm excited about the job you have open."*

Of course, these answers work only if you've been in your current job long enough for them to make sense. If you've been there for just, say, six months, saying that you're looking for new challenges is going to sound bad—like you have unrealistic expectations and get bored way too easily. In that case, you generally need to be more frank about what's driving you to look so soon. For example:

- *"I was hired to help write healthcare policy because of my past work with Congress, but it's turned out that they really need someone with a more scientific background. That's not me, so I'm looking for something that's a better fit."*

- *"One of the main reasons I took the job is that I was accepted to work with the manager who hired me. However, she left right after I started, and I'm getting the sense that the department is going in a direction that isn't as strong a fit for me."*

Five Interview Turn-Offs to Avoid

1. **Being too early.** You probably (hopefully) know you shouldn't be late to an interview, but did you know there's such a thing as being too early? If you show up more than five or ten minutes early, you may annoy your interviewer, who may feel obligated to interrupt what she's doing in order to greet you. Leaving yourself a buffer so that you don't arrive late is good—but if you get to the location early, kill the extra time at a coffee shop or even in your car rather than walking in more than ten minutes before your scheduled appointment.

2. **Underdressing.** In the vast majority of industries, you need to wear a suit to a job interview. Even many offices with a business casual dress code still expect candidates to wear a suit. The best approach, though, is to know the norms for interview dress for *your own field*. And not just your field in general, but your field in your particular geographic area, since the norms for your field in California might be different from its norms in Boston. If you're not sure of the particular norms that might be in play, default to wearing a suit.

3. **Addressing only one of your interviewers.** If you're being interviewed by more than one person at a time, make sure that you're addressing and making eye contact with all of them as you talk. Sometimes candidates address only the person they think is the most important or more senior interviewer, which can come across as quite rude and dismissive.

4. **Minimizing concerns about your fit for the job.** If your interviewer observes that you haven't had experience with a key part of the job, don't dismiss it by claiming that you can learn anything or you're sure it won't be a challenge for you. Good interviewers don't want a sales pitch; they want to see that you have a realistic view of the job's challenges, and they will appreciate an honest conversation about how you'll approach those challenges.

5. **Being so formal that the interviewer can't get a sense of who you are.** Sometimes people get so hung up on the formality of interviews that they

become so stiff or reserved that it's impossible to get a real sense of what they'd be like as a coworker day to day—which can leave the interviewer unsure of who they'd really be hiring. You of course don't want to treat the interviewer like a close friend whom you've known forever, but you do want to let your personality show. Think of the way you'd conduct yourself in a meeting with a coworker whom you see a few times a month and have a warm relationship with. That's the tone to strive for here.

14. You know that your old manager will probably give you a bad reference

If you know that a previous boss is likely to give you a bad reference, the first thing to do is to figure out how likely it is that the person will be contacted by a reference checker. Many employers will contact only the references you provide, so you might be able to simply leave that person off the list. However, it's possible that a reference checker will ask why that manager isn't on your list—especially if it's the manager from your most recent job—and may specifically ask to be put in touch with the person.

If that's the case, don't just connect them without giving some context for what they're likely to hear. For example:

- *"I want to be up-front with you that my relationship with Jorge was a difficult one. We didn't see eye to eye on strategy, which is one of the reasons I left, and I think he was looking for a very different type of work than what I do. But I'd be glad to put you in touch with other people from that job who could give you a different perspective on my work there, including the department VP, who I had a great relationship with."* (If you don't have a VP to offer up, even offering a peer or two can be reassuring to a reference checker. In fact, sometimes the mere offer of others can nudge them to take the bad input with a healthy amount of skepticism.)

- *"I should tell you in advance that I'm not sure what kind of reference you'll get from Lucy. She had a pretty volatile style, and some days she loved my work and other days she didn't. That was her style with everyone, not just me, and I know she gave some unflattering references to people who were known to have done great work. So I can put you in touch with her, but I'd ask that you take the reference with a heavy grain of salt. I'd be glad to put you in touch with other people I worked with at that job, though."*

The biggest key to neutralizing a bad reference is to provide plenty of other references who will speak glowingly of you—so make sure you do that!

15. Employer wants to call your current boss for a reference, but your boss doesn't know you're looking

It's very common to interview without telling your current employer that you're looking for a new job. That's because tipping off your boss that you plan to leave can result in your being pushed out earlier than you intended to go.

Normally, the employers who you're interviewing with should understand this, and will be sensitive to the fact that you don't want to jeopardize your current job. However, in some cases you might encounter an employer who pushes to be allowed to contact your current employer anyway. If that happens, here's how to push back:

- *"My current employer doesn't know that I'm thinking of leaving, and telling them before I've accepted an offer could jeopardize my job there. I can't risk that, but I'd be happy to supply other references who can tell you about my work."*

- *"I can't put my current job in jeopardy by letting them know I'm looking before I've accepted another offer. But I can give you plenty of other references, and if this is a sticking point, one option is that we could have any offer be contingent on a good reference from them—but I'd want to work out the offer details first to make sure that we're able to agree on terms before you call them."*

16. Interviewer mentions that she knows your current boss

If you're looking for a new job but haven't told your current boss (which is a completely normal thing to keep to yourself), you're probably going to have a moment of panic if your interviewer reveals that she knows your manager. Is she going to mention your interview to your boss? Wasn't this supposed to be confidential? Aggh.

Don't panic. Calmly and directly explain that your boss doesn't know that you're looking, and ask your interviewer to keep your conversation confidential:

- *"I haven't mentioned to Jane that I'm talking with you, and I'd prefer to keep my job search confidential for now. Can I ask you to keep our conversation between us?"*

Optional add-on, if it's true:

- *"Jane is great, but our company tends to push people out quickly if it comes out that they're talking with other companies, so it's important to me to keep this confidential."*

17. You know you've flubbed the interview

Walking out of an interview knowing that you flubbed it is a terrible feeling! And it might make you wonder if there's any way to get a do-over or otherwise acknowledge to the interviewer that you know you weren't at your best.

For what it's worth, I've talked to a lot of people who thought they flubbed answers and still ended up getting the job. Some questions don't matter nearly as much as others, and sometimes people's self-assessments are just off.

But if you're convinced your interview was a disaster, you have a few different options for how to handle it.

If you feel you just messed up on a question or two, as opposed to the entire interview, you could send the interviewer a thank-you note that reiterates your interest in the job and says something like this:

- *"I realized after we spoke that when you asked me about X, I should have said _____. I realized afterward that I'd misunderstood the question and wanted to correct it!"*

If the issue is that the interviewer asked a lot of questions in an area you're not as strong in, you could say something like this in your thank-you note:

- *"I want to be up-front about the fact that I don't have a lot of experience in X, although I do think that my background in Y would be really useful in helping you achieve Z."* (But keep in mind that if they're really looking for serious experience in X, this may not be a job you'll succeed in—which means it's a job you don't want.)

If you were just having an off day (didn't sleep the night before, dealing with bad personal news, recovering from illness, or some such), and you're sure it impacted you in ways the interviewer picked up on, you can say something like this:

- *"I want to be transparent that I wasn't at my best when we spoke, due to a relatively sleepless night the night before. If we have the chance to talk again, I hope you'll see the difference!"* (But do be sure that the interviewer would have picked up on it before saying this—if not, this can be a surprising note to receive.)

Will any of this make a difference? Maybe, maybe not. It really depends on the interviewer's assessment, what they care about most and what they're de-prioritizing, and what the rest of the candidate pool is like. But it's worth a shot.

18. Interviewer asks you to do free work

It's smart for employers to find ways to see job candidates in action by using tools like writing tests, problem-solving simulations, and (short) mock projects, as long as these requests don't take a significant amount of time and are only being used for assessment purposes. But it's not cool for an employer to ask you to do something that will require a significant amount of your time (more than an hour or two) or that they might actually use.

If an employer asks you to spend more than an hour or two producing real work for them, you're in a tricky position, since if you push back, you risk being taken out of the running. Because of that, this comes down to how comfortable you are with that possibility. One way to look at it is that you wouldn't want to work for a company that's inconsiderate of candidates— or worse, takes advantage of them—but the reality is that not everyone has the luxury of having lots of options.

If you do decide to push back, here are some ways to say it:

- *"I don't think I'll be able to do this project justice without knowing a lot more. We could talk about doing it as a consulting project if you'd like, but because of other commitments right now I can't really spend more than an hour or so on an assessment exercise. But I could do* (name a much smaller piece of the task) *to give you a feel for my work if that would be helpful to you?"*

- *"I don't usually do spec work, but I can definitely send you examples of similar work that I've done in the past."*

My interviewer keeps asking me to help with her work

A reader writes:

I have a unique skill set within HR and I have recently been interviewing for a job at a new company. The direc-

tor who I have interviewed with is clearly under water and doesn't know how to proceed with the work that I would be doing, should they hire me for the position. Since my initial interview, she has scheduled one conference call and sent two emails full of questions for me to answer to "help her out" as she navigates her new role. (The conference call was to prep her for a meeting where she wasn't sure what to ask, and I had to provide her with basically an education on international HR deployments and new market entry outside the U.S. The next set of questions was to clarify things she didn't understand from that meeting.) Yesterday, she sent me a list of questions because they are trying to set up an international benefits plan and she had a lot of questions about what kind of plan to select, how it should be administered, etc.

This puts me in a terrible position because I don't want to seem like I am not a team player or willing to help, but clearly I am not an employee and they have made no offer, so I feel she is really taking advantage of the situation.

I have a second interview coming up, and the recruiter keeps telling me to "hang in there." I don't want to keep this up unless I have an offer, but I am not sure how to step away without jeopardizing this career opportunity. Thoughts?

She is indeed taking advantage of the situation, and it's not okay to ask you to help her with her work without compensation.

It's true that a strong interview process will include finding ways to see candidates in action, using exercises, simulations, or real-life problems to see what their work is like. But that's not what this is; it's an unethical grab for free help, whether she realizes it or not. (To be clear, it's quite possible that she doesn't realize she's doing anything wrong—she needs help, you seem friendly and knowledgeable, and she probably hasn't thought beyond that. That doesn't make it okay, but it might help to think of it as ineptness on her part rather than anything nefarious.)

As for how to handle it, you have a few options:

1. Talk to the recruiter and explain you feel uncomfortable with what you're being asked to do. The recruiter might be able to relay that message in a way that doesn't damage your chances. (Don't do this if your recruiter seems ham-fisted, though; she'd need to be able to act with some nuance here.)

2. Be unavailable to help rather than refusing outright: "Unfortunately I'm at a seminar / traveling / slammed with work all this week. I know you need timely answers and I don't want to hold you up."

3. Point her to other resources: "The XYZ Association website is a great source of information on this stuff—you should find a lot of what you're looking for there." (You can do this in combination with suggestion 2, too.)

4. Frame it as consulting work: "This is a pretty involved topic, and one that needs more than a five-minute conversation. Would it make sense to set up a short-term consulting agreement?" (Be aware, though, that this risks her flouncing off in irritation, thinking "I was just asking for a few minutes of her time!" and harming your candidacy as a result. That's entirely unfair, but it happens.)

Of course, you could also just be direct ("I feel uncomfortable helping with this when I'm not yet working for you"), but it can be tough to pull that off without causing tension, and you don't want to cause tension in this particular relationship right now. And you have other options (see above), so I'd go with one of those. Good luck!

19. You've had multiple interviews with a company with no end to the process in sight

It's increasingly common for employers to ask candidates to interview more than once before they make a hiring decision. From the employer side of things, I think it's a good trend, because hiring someone after a single one-hour conversation can be risky, especially with more senior jobs. But that should generally mean two or three meetings—not ten.

If you find yourself in a long interview process with no indication of when it will end, it's entirely reasonable to say something like this:

- *"Can you tell me more about what steps remain in your process and what your likely timeline will be for making a decision?"*

- *"I'm very interested in this position, but it's becoming harder for me to take time off work for additional meetings. Would it be possible for us to consolidate some of the remaining steps?"*

20. Asking if the employer will cover travel expenses for an out-of-town interview

Some employers cover travel expenses for out-of-town candidates to come in for an interview, and others don't. It also can vary by industry and by the level of position (you're more likely to get expenses covered when interviewing for a senior role). Often, employers will mention their travel policy right up front when inviting you to interview, but some don't think to mention it.

If you're invited to interview out of state, it's completely fine and normal to ask about expense reimbursement. Say it this way:

- *"I'd love to come out for an interview. How do you normally handle travel expenses?"*

If it turns out that the invitation doesn't include travel expenses, you'll need to decide whether you're interested enough in the job—and think you're a strong enough candidate—to make the expense worth it to you. If you haven't already had a phone interview with this employer, you could ask to do that first (since that stage may reveal a mismatch on either side and save you a needless investment of time and money). You can ask for that this way:

- *"I'm very interested in the job and would be willing to cover my own expenses, but would it be possible for us to conduct a phone interview first to make sure that we're a strong match?"*

21. You realize during a job interview that there's no way you'd take the job

In general, if you realize during an interview that you don't want the job, it still makes sense to stay and finish the interview. Even though you don't want this job, it's possible that the company might have an opening in the future that you *will* want, so it's to your advantage to finish, make a good impression, and not be remembered as the person who suddenly short-circuited the interview.

However, there are some cases where it does make sense to cut things short, such as if you're in the middle of an all-day interview or if your interviewer is outright abusive. In that case, say something like:

- *"As we're talking, I'm realizing that this probably isn't quite the right fit for me. I really appreciate the time you've spent talking with me, but I don't feel right taking up more of your day."*

If there's a reason that you're comfortable sharing, ideally you'd include that, too. For example, you might say "I'm looking for something more ___" or "I hadn't realized the job was so heavily focused on ___" or "We're farther apart on salary than I'd realized." That way, they might think of you in the future if they have an opening that would be a better match.

But if the reason is "You seem like a horrible jerk," then just stick with the less specific language above, since there's very little payoff in saying that (other than perhaps extreme gratification in the moment).

22. Asking for your own office, to work from home, or for other perks

Theoretically, you can negotiate anything as part of a job offer. In practice, what you're able to negotiate will depend on how much leverage you have, and that's a function of how much the employer wants to hire you and how in demand your skills are. If you're relatively junior in your career, you won't have much negotiating leverage. But as you become more senior and build your reputation, you'll gain the standing to ask for more. That doesn't mean you'll get it, of course—but it becomes more reasonable to ask.

Of course, the "reasonable" part is key. You need to have a sense of what the norms are in your field and at your level, so that you can calibrate the request accordingly.

It helps to frame the request as "Would you be open to X?" or "I'd like Y because of Z. Is that an option on your end?" That way you're being direct about what you want, but you're not demanding it like a crazed prima donna.

As part of negotiating the offer, say something like this:

- Asking about working from home: *"My current job is very work-from-home-friendly, and I usually work from home a few times a month. Would you be open to my continuing to do that?"*

   Sometimes it's easier to negotiate working from home when you explicitly connect it to the salary: *"I understand you're not able to go up to $Y. I'd be willing to accept the job for $X if I could work from home one day a week, since there's value to me in cutting back on commuting time. Would that work on your end?"*

- Asking about office space: *"Can you tell me about where I'd be working? Would I be in a private office or a shared space?"* If the person tells you that it will be a shared space, you can say, *"Would it be possible to have a private office? This type of work often requires concentration, and I've found that having a quiet space lets me focus and get more done."* (Keep in mind that the answer will likely be subject to factors like whether space is even available and whether it will cause issues with people above you who don't have their own space—but you can pose the question.)

23. Answering questions about your salary history when this job would mean a big jump in pay

Ideally, you'd never discuss your current salary or your salary history with prospective employers. Your earnings are none of their business, and they should be able to figure out what to pay for a role without needing your personal financial information.

In reality, though, many employers insist on knowing what you've been earning, and will sometimes use that information to lower the salary they offer you. If that's the case, the best thing to do is to address it head-on:

- *"One of the main reasons I'm looking to change jobs is that I know I'm underpaid for the field. I'm leaving in part to get my salary back in line with market rates—meaning $X–$Y for a job like this one."*

- *"I accepted my current job knowing that it paid significantly below market because I loved the organization and was excited for the chance to learn a huge amount working with some great mentors. But now I've built up my expertise and I'm ready to move into a new stage of my career, and am leaving in part in order to be paid in line with the market."*

I said something very close to that second one early in my career—and doubled my salary as a result. I had been working for a nonprofit that paid very low salaries, which was fine with me at the time because I loved the organization and I loved my work. But when I was interviewing for my next job, it came out that the salary I was asking for was more than double what I'd been making. The interviewer asked me why she should give me such a big increase, and I said something like:

- *"I've loved the work I've been doing, and I was willing to do it for well below market rates because I was so personally invested in the organization and I was learning a huge amount that I wouldn't have had the chance to learn somewhere else. But now I'm ready to move on from that stage, and part of the reason I'm leaving is because I want to be paid a normal market rate."*

It worked!

24. Asking what a job pays before embarking on a lengthy hiring process or traveling for an out-of-town interview

Employers like to play coy on salary, and you can sometimes end up going through a multistep interview process without ever learning what the job pays.

But while there's a convention that job candidates shouldn't bring up salary first (which is ridiculous and outdated, but still persists), it *is* more accepted to ask about salary before making a significant investment of time during the hiring process. If you're being asked to travel out of town, take significant time off work, or set up multiple interviews on different days, employers are more likely to understand that you first want to make sure that you're in the same salary ballpark. And really, that's in the employer's interest too; it doesn't make any sense to spend significant time with each other, only to find out later that there's no way they could afford you.

Here are some ways to say it:

- *"Before you pay for my travel, can we touch base on the salary range for the position so that we can make sure we're in the same ballpark?"*

- *"I hope you don't mind my asking at this stage, but because it's difficult for me to take time off work to interview, are you able to give me a sense of the salary range so that we can make sure we're in the same ballpark before we move forward?"*

- *"Since it sounds as if your hiring process has a number of steps—which I think is a smart way to hire—could we touch base on the salary range before moving forward, so that I'm not using up your time if we're not in the same ballpark?"*

25. You haven't heard back from your interviewer

It's common for the hiring process to take far longer than candidates expect it to—and even far longer than employers tell you they'll need. In fact, when interviewers tell you that you'll hear back within a particular time frame, it's smart to mentally double or triple it.

But if you're getting antsy and want to know where things stand, and if it's at least a few days past the timeline they gave you (and preferably more like a week past it), it's fine to reach out and ask for an update:

- *"I wanted to check in with you and see if you have an updated timeline for making a decision about the X position."*

Don't freak out, though, if you don't hear anything back for a while. Many employers won't take the time to get back to candidates until they have something firm to report: an offer or a rejection. And inexplicably, many employers leave people hanging indefinitely, not even bothering to send rejection letters to people who took the time to come in to interview. Because of that, if you don't hear from the employer after you've followed up once, the best thing you can do is to put the job out of your mind and move on . . . and let it be a pleasant surprise if they do get back in touch.

26. Negotiating salary

People often think that negotiating salary means presenting a formal case to justify why they're worth more money than the employer has initially offered. The thing to know about salary negotiation is that most of the time, that's not at all necessary! Often you can get more money just by saying something like this:

- *"I'm really excited about this job, but I was hoping the salary would be higher. Would you be able to go up to $X?"*

- *"I was hoping you'd be able to go up to $X. Is that possible?"*

- *"Do you have any flexibility on the salary? The number I had in mind is $X."*

- *"If you were able to do $X, I'd be thrilled to accept."*

Important: After you say one of these, *stop talking*. Even if you're nervous or uncomfortable or mentally freaking out about what the hiring manager will say, once you've made the request, stop talking and wait. There might be an awkward pause, and that's okay. Eventually the hiring manager will speak, and you want to wait for that to happen—because if you keep talking, you may end up undercutting yourself simply to ease the awkwardness of the silence.

27. You realize you wildly overshot the salary range

One of the many reasons that talking about salary with prospective employers is anxiety-producing is that you don't want to undercut yourself by naming a number lower than what the employer would pay, but you also don't want to name a number so high that they decide they can't afford you and take you out of the running when you really would have accepted something lower.

Broadly speaking, the best way to avoid this is to do your research on salary beforehand, so that the number you name is rooted in solid knowledge of the market in your field and your geographic area.

But if you find yourself in a situation where you realize that the number you named is far outside the employer's budget and you'd actually be willing to take a lower salary, try one of these:

- *"Can you tell me the range you had in mind? I'm interested enough in the role that I'd be willing to be flexible on salary if everything else in the offer is right."*

- *"I'd be willing to consider that salary level because I'm so excited about the job itself* (or because I know it will be necessary to change fields, or whatever else applies)."

- *"I have to be honest—I'm new to the area* (or field) *and still refining my information about salary ranges. $X isn't prohibitive for me, so I'd love to keep talking if you're still interested."*

28. Interviewer pushes you to accept a job offer on the spot

Good interviewers won't push you to accept a job offer on the spot. They might *hope* that you will, so that they can wrap up the process, but they'll understand that it's a big decision for you to make and that it's perfectly understandable for you to want some time to think it over.

If an employer is pushing you for an immediate answer, say this:

- *"Thank you so much. I'm really interested in the job. Can I take some time to think it over and figure out if I have any questions, and give you an answer by Friday?"* (In most cases it's reasonable to ask for anywhere from a few days to a week.)

If you're pressed beyond that, you can simply say:

- *"It's a big decision, and while I'm very excited about the job, I want to make sure that I've thought everything over and that I don't have any outstanding questions."*

Also, note that you generally should *not* say things like "I'm waiting to hear back from another employer"— employers want to believe they're your first choice.

29. Letting your first-choice employer know that you have another offer

If you're interviewing with multiple employers and get an offer from one before your first choice has made a decision, don't panic. If you reach out to your first choice and explain the situation, they may be able to expedite things on their end—if they're interested enough.

Contact the employer you're most interested in immediately (don't delay by even a day!) and say this:

- *"I'm extremely interested in the job with you. I know you're still moving through your process, but I've just received an offer from another company and I need to give them my decision within a week. You're my first choice and I'd much prefer the job with you, but I'm constricted by their timeline. Is there any chance of hearing back from you with a definite decision by Monday?"*

If they're very interested in you, they'll do what they can to move up their process. Or if nothing else, they'll at least let you know that they don't expect to be able to make a decision that quickly, and then you can factor that information into how you proceed.

30. Turning down an offer

You got the job! And . . . you've decided you don't want it. Maybe you can't come to terms on salary, or maybe you got an even better offer somewhere else, or maybe you just realized that the job isn't quite the right match for you.

If you're stressing about how to turn down the offer, know that people do it all the time. It's a normal part of doing business, and a good employer isn't going to be shocked or outraged. You're just as allowed to turn down an offer as an employer is allowed to turn you down for a job.

So just be straightforward. Say, for example:

• *"Thank you so much for the offer. I really appreciate the time you spent talking with me, but after giving it a lot of thought, I'm going to decline the offer. I've realized I want to get back to doing more original research, which I know wouldn't be a focus for this role. But I think you're doing great work, and I hope we might have the chance to talk again sometime in the future."*

- *"I really appreciate your being straightforward with me about the salary limits. I think we're too far apart on salary, so I'm going to have to decline the offer. But I'm really grateful to have had the chance to get to know your company, and I wish you all the best in the work you're doing."*

Conclusion

What I hope you'll take away from this book is that you can and should speak up when something is bothering you or you're hoping something can be handled differently. Speaking up doesn't have to mean alienating people or causing tension in your relationships; you can be direct without being rude, and you can be assertive without being disagreeable.

And in fact, while this is a book about how to have difficult conversations at work, I've heard from many readers over the years that the type of advice we've covered here translates to other realms as well—family, friendships, dating, and significant others.

Some of the principles from this book that you can apply in any part of your life are:

- Be direct. Don't expect people to read your mind and then stew when they don't. Do yourself *and the other person* the favor of speaking up when you're hoping someone will do something differently. Candor, as long as it's mixed with kindness, will usually lead you someplace good.

- If you've spoken up about something a few times and not seen any change, stop addressing the individual instances ("You did X again") and talk about the big picture instead ("We've talked a bunch of times about the problems X causes for me, but it keeps happening— how can we handle this differently?").

- Assume goodwill on the part of the other person. You'll generally get much better results if you approach the other person in a collaborative way rather than thinking of the person as your adversary.

- You can acknowledge that others might see things differently than you do and respect their right to that point of view, while still being clear about what you need.

- Take criticism gracefully, even if you disagree. Even if you mull it over and conclude that the feedback is groundless, it will still help you learn how someone else sees you, and that can be valuable.

- You can say almost anything if you've established yourself as a kind, considerate, and transparent person.

Of course, no one gets this stuff right every time. (I certainly don't, as my family, friends, and past coworkers undoubtedly can attest.) But if you're clear in your head that this is what you're striving for in your relationships, you're more likely to get the outcomes you want, more of the time. Speaking up—respectfully but directly—will help you have a happier, more satisfying, and less stressful life, at work and outside it.

Acknowledgments

A number of people helped make this book possible. Particular thanks go to all the folks at Ballantine, especially my wonderful editor, Sara Weiss; my endlessly patient agent, Heather Flaherty; Janet Burkitt, who both lends me ideas and makes me laugh loudly in inappropriate venues; Jenny Green, who was my very first reader and even claimed to like what she read; Marty Higareda, who has spent way too much time just seeing the top of my head bent over a computer and never complained; and both my parents, who taught me to speak up for myself and deeply regretted it soon after.